GATEWAY TO MUSH

Thoughts and poems by
Brett Lars Underwood

Spartan
Press

Spartan Press

Kansas City, Missouri

Spartan
Press

Copyright © Brett Underwood, 2024
First Edition: 1 3 5 7 9 10 8 6 4 2
ISBN: 978-1-958182-74-1
LCCN: 2024940596

Cover image: Jerome Gaynor
Author photo: Chris Johnson

Acknowledgments

Special thanks to the editors of these publications, where these poems first appeared (in some form or another):

52ndcity.com, *The Gasconade Review presents: STRANGE GODS OF THE PRAIRIE*, *The Gasconade Review presents: MISSOURI IS A GHOST-SHAPED THING*, *THE COSMIC LOST AND FOUND: An Anthology of Missouri Poets* (Spartan Press), *AFTER THE FLOOD: Paintings by Greg Edmondson; Words by Others* (Stubborn Mule Press), *Bruxism 10*, *PoetryBay.com*, *SCUZZ REPORT*

"Pootie Tang and John Cage" is on the The Pat Sajak Assassins latest album "Sounds Like Technology" as "Agent Underwood"

Table of Contents:

Thank you to the dingus that kept the door open
and let me in. You know, ol' what'isname.
Also, thanks to:
Aaron Belz
Richard Byrne
Matthew Scott Freeman
and
Stefene Russell
for looking this over and offering their expertise.

"The one thing that everybody wants is to be free...
not to be managed, threatened, directed, restrained,
obliged, fearful, administered, they want none of these
things they all want to feel free, the word discipline, and
forbidden and investigated and imprisoned brings horror
and fear into all hearts, they do not want to be afraid
not more than is necessary in the ordinary business of
living where one has to earn one's living and has to fear
want and disease and death....The only thing that any
one wants now is to be free, to be let alone, to live their
life as they can, but not to be watched, controlled and
scared, no no, not."

-Gertrude Stein, *Wars I Have Seen*

"This place has only three exits, sir: Madness, and Death."

-René Daumal, *A Night of Serious Drinking*

"I do not understand why, when I ask for grilled lobster
in a restaurant, I'm never served a cooked telephone."

-Salvador Dalí

A PREFACE APLENTY

Find the journals scribbled in darkest hours, long ago.
A glimmer of light, too, when wandering and wondering
about how to make it in the world after the small-town
Existentialism-gone-to-university theology, sports
failure and injury and the re-education on the streets and
in the alleys of St. Louis that have always been about
"who you know."

Fucking nepotism.

Thankfully there are weirdos and music; art and other
forms of expression, plus a bunch of "foreign" in...
flu...ences to explore. Not too deep, but just say that
beings of a younger age will either face the bullshit of
this community and figure it out or will stay in isolation
and belch bullshit. Belch plenty of it. Revel in it. BUT...
(maybe this is wrong) figure out a way to connect without
these isolated tweets and complaints and grumpy vibes.

Sound weird here, but, think of something positive
to emit. Even weirder, breathe deep when freaking out.
Love a spot on a wall as an image. As an homage to self,
breathe in and out. Find a park and escape the head.
Give self up.

Need a bodyguard? Find one, but find a place to give
up I mean, give up. You are not your ego. Your haircut.
Your friends. Your sex life. Your taste in music or food
or blip blop bling.

Spend time in libraries for days reading and realizing
that people still do this instead of crapping into FB.
Depressed? Walk to another library or a tree. Perch upon
a rock and read a book or keep walking. Go to a theatre
and sit and wait. If that doesn't work, contact a friend.

The darkness in our society can be overcome by love and creativity. Reason won't cure doubt. The mind doesn't hold the best of consciousness. The answers aren't held in apparent solutions. It all seems hopeless, but you should know that wisdom lies in between two entities: that what you know and that what you are afraid to know.

Blah Blah Blah.

Nothing matters.

Breathe.

Walk.

Pass the time.

Feel it.

Kiss the knower of the power of beats and the reader of the Beats. Thank the jazzman who knows the bicycle and how to make music out of wind. Make it in St. Louis. Thanks for reading.

This book is a culmination of years of journaling, pondering and freewriting. Part of my existence has been late-night radio and the booking of, hosting and attending thousands of music, art and poetry events. The title reflects this in such a subtle manner to the point that I wondered whether it was "too inside," but there it is *GATEWAY TO MUSH*. Years ago, the incredible band, Grand Ulena, released an album called "Gateway to Dignity." They were a band that I played a lot on KDHX in the middle-of-the night. They made an influence.

Then, of course, there is the whole "Gateway to the West" thing. Oh! How about "gateway drug"?

Yes, I've had many experiences that were gateways to writing and some of the pieces in the book were written years ago, before the publication of my first book, *MUSH*.

This message will dissolve in 5-4-3-2-1—1—2-3-4-5...

GATEWAY TO MUSH

THINGS THE SIDEWALKS SAY

The sidewalks say, "This is the city."
The sidewalks say you aren't there yet.
They say your car is around the corner.
The sidewalks say, "Your feet hurt."
They say you're tired.
The sidewalks say you could use some grass.
They say, "Crack, crack, crack, crack."

The sidewalks say there are better things than asphalt.
They say, "One step at a time."
The sidewalks tell you to pick up your feet
They say, "Your shoelaces have seen better days."
The sidewalks say that these worms won't survive this heat.
They say the ants are hard at work.

The sidewalks say, "Pick it up!"
They say this is the structure.
The sidewalks say that these roots are powerful.
The sidewalks say birds shit, dogs shit, mud and hair weaves.
They say, "This is what used to be called a dime bag.
The sidewalks say, "You're trippin'."
They say, "Crack, crack, crack, crack."

The sidewalks say you should talk a walk.
They say "Hear the secrets,"
The sidewalks say these buildings have basements.
They say, "These buildings have weaknesses."
The sidewalks say you want to know.
They say, "Fuck television. Fuck cellphones. Fuck it. Fuck it."

The sidewalks say there is blood in the streets.
They say there is blood in the soil.
The sidewalks say, "There is injustice."
They say the guy at the corner store knows
The sidewalks know the truth.
The sidewalks say, "Wait."

The sidewalks say that you don't know the truth.
They say you don't want to.
The sidewalks are mocking you.
The sidewalks say, "Go home and watch the footage."
The sidewalks have the dirt.

The sidewalks are a cover.
The sidewalks say, "I will bring you to a place of
forgiveness."
They say that they know your hunger.
They say the longing is only a symptom.
They say that you can overcome this.
The sidewalks say, "Crack. Crack. Crack. Crack."

The sidewalks say you could do better.
They say, "You missed the bus."
The sidewalks say you will be better.
They say you're loved.
They say, "Fuck that asshole."
They say there's always tomorrow.
They say there's nothing more than this.

The sidewalks say that the leaves hide your shadow.
The sidewalks say, "Look at the eclipse."
They say you're not everything.

They say there's no apocalypse.
They say you are you.
They say, "Crack. Crack. Crack. Crack."

The sidewalks say there is something lurking.
They say you never know.
The sidewalks say the meter's running.
They say your luck is up.
They say, "Follow the money."
They say, "Crack. Crack. Crack. Crack."

The sidewalks say there's no use in running.
The sidewalks say, "Fight inside the belly of the beast."
They say, "You got this."
They say, "You know the truth."
They say, "These buildings are going to fall."
They say that this too will pass.
They say that you're overthinking it.
They say you're trippin'.
They say, "I'm harder than you."
They say, "I'm better than the streets."
They say, "Crack. Crack. Crack. Crack."

The sidewalks say that this is philosophy.
They say that they will bring friends.
They say that they will discover enemies.
They say they will bring you promise.
They say, "Go to the park."
They say, "It's not worth it."
They say, "God is strange."
They say, "Did you see that shit!"
They say, "Crack. Crack Crack Crack."

ORGANIZATION

He is weary of madness on parade. The Feng shui isn't
    working today.
He's tired of stepping on it all and being the behemoth
    in his space.
He stacks the detritus all along the walls, sits down
    and stares at the page.
He writes:

A vista.
Clear a view through a cluster of clambering
    nincompoopery.
A walk amidst birds and trees and turn-of-the-century
    urban landscaping.
The lungs of the city and frayed shoestrings commingle
    and shuffle.
Sunshine and dilated pupils. Dreamy clouds form dreams…
    lots of dreams.
Dreams of order. Dreams of silence. Dreams of daydreams
    of sleep and bliss
in nightmares of clouds.

While breeze brushes the grass into nothing but park grass
    and manmade wonder and:
"Mommy," the little girl says, "why do some of these trees
    look plastic?"
"Well, Jenny," the Mommy says, "That's an interesting
    question.
But maybe more interesting is the question: Why are some
    trees made out of plastic?"

A police helicopter hovers over a nearby neighborhood.

"The Previl wears Dada," sings the little girl.

"What?!" says the mother.

"Daddy says that when Rosy walks into the room."

"Don't make me slap you again."

"Oh, Mommy!"

There was pause exemplified by a space in this page.

And then another one.

"Mommy, what's an orgasm?"

A diesel powered leaf blower drowns the breeze of
    thought.

"I need to go to the mall."

"Not again, Mommy! What's dada?!" the little girl says.

"The first word that came out of your mouth," the
    mother sighs.

"Rosy thinks our house is shit," says the little girl.

The mother yanks the girl by the arm and walks her out
of the park to the parking garage in her mind. They drive
24 miles to a shopping mall. There is a black cat in a
camouflage hoodie holding a sign that reads, "Waiting
    for MODOT."

The clouds formed into "Got MILF?" and the mother
    begins to cry yesterday's tears.

She decides to buy shoes.

Lots of shoes.

He sighs and conceives airtight boxes housed in many-shelved units but can't find his hammer. He takes a majestic dump and decides to take a very long walk during which he kicks a soda can for some time.

DOG

Your malodorous heel
has not the appeal
of the dish you'll offer tonight.
When we finish this walk
on asphalt and rock
I'll hold back the strong urge to bite.

You're a nine-o'clock shadow
by the time you come home
to spring me from out of your cage.
Still, I'll act like your bitch
and comfort your itch for rough licks
and love without rage.

IT'S TUESDAY MORNING

This is the kind of morning
when the garbage truck
would shatter our minds
because we left the window
open.

This is the kind of morning
when I would get up
to take a piss
and freak out for a few minutes
until I located my wallet,
keys and stepped outside
to locate the sled.

This is the kind of morning
when I'd return to bed
with two bottles of beer
and drizzle some on your belly
before I went down.

This is the kind of morning
when the boom box was next
to the mattress
and I would run my finger
across the knob up and down the dial
until you woke up
and needed to hear
MY LIFE WITH THE THRILL KILL KULT
to warm you up

And it DID!

This is the kind of morning
when you flipped out
coming back from the can
"Where's the boa!
Where's the fucking boa constrictor!
The fucking window is open!
The garbage truck!
The dumpster is right down there!
Oh Fuck!
Oh Fuck!
Brian is going to kill me!"

This is the kind of morning
when I would march through ten
inches of snow
to be with you;
when you called on the landline
and cried about your night.

This is the kind of morning
when your ex would be banging
on the front door
which was easy enough to ignore
from the bedroom in the back
but banging on the window just
behind the curtain?

Wow!

I said, "I thought I was your back door man."

You said, "The future's uncertain and the end
is always near."
I felt it and so did you with each thrust
to the beat of his fists on wood, glass and steel
punctuating the muffled giggles.

This is the kind of morning
I think about waking solo
on the unforgiving futon,
scrolling through whatever
fucking videos that were hilarious
in the schmoke of last night.
On this kind of morning,
I'm not sure what to do
but smash up some garlic.
Cook some beans.
Boil and fry some eggs and pork.

Rain coming, so I might skip the walk
on neuropathetic trails

Oh, here's an avocado.
The rain hits the windows gently.
Maybe some Terry Riley
and a nap,
scrolling through memories
of morning's like this.

KNEES KNOCK

Maybe I dreamt that I heard this delivered at the top of somebody's lungs. The stage— a street corner or a bus stop, perhaps. Or an ice-cream truck on a pretty day. Or squawking out of one of those storm-warning blasters that wake me up from time-to-time. I thought it might be funny to replace the dial tone with this rant, but somebody would charge far too much jingle for this jangle, so here it is in script:

* * *

"Shut the Fuck Up!
We're trying to make some music down here! Jive-Ass Mother Fuckers."

-John Zorn, August 1997...to Czech Republic president Vaclav Havel, U.S. Secretary of State Madeleine Albright, Laurie Anderson and Lou Reed, who were talking during a Bar Kokhba show at The Knitting Factory.

* * *

Their encroachment sometimes welcome, sometimes haunting can send a grown man to the john, the pulpit, the confessional, the madhouse. The same goes for all beings.

Lhasa Apso yelp. Wolves bay. A car explodes. Little kitty cats mew.

Daddy's got a squeezebox. Mommy cries herself to sleep.
Karin is crazed by cuckoos in the night.

11

The blech blondes poppalop and blabber in the
venues while the pizzicato and the strummers die in the
idiocy of Listerine strips and clogged up ears.
It can be an absolute torment. People think they've got
freight trains running through their head between cotton
balls and ear plugs.

Bob saves up for a parabolic microphone with the tips he
makes washing sedan windshields with a squeegee. Frank
apes ducks from a blind, though he is deaf. Boom boom
chug chug munch munch.

          No silence. Plunging needles perhaps
or popping pills to bring peace. But no silence.
        The buzz continues.
           Din.
      "…and nobody knows sound like me.
Nobody knows sound. I hate sound and wear earplugs to
work to sleep to everything so I don't have to wear that
sound, Man!" said the perturbed technician.
      Postal workers hum and groan delivering checks
to pay for the buffering and the AC units drown out the
crimes of the night.
      Love and happiness conquer the banal screams
of youths and during the winter months even Bach and
Beethoven are muffled in the roar of the heaters, blowing
their suffocating breath to keep the anemic from teeth
chatters and shivers. A well-placed bug captures the ensuing
moans but can never take from her the past dalliances of
the night and the voices for which she yearns. He'll never
say, "I love you." He doesn't speak English. He thinks she
just want the bang bang.

Ashamed of her lisp, he mutters to himself as he backs away each morning, when the sickness is at its most audible.

The coffee maker percolates to the ticking of the clock.

The wrinkle of the sheets recalls the nightmare and a swift machete
  to the femoral artery of problems with Mama.

The Sawtooth Mountains invite Morricone to the piazza and the nuns beg their pupils to cease before the whack, whack, whack of the rulers on bones. The couple upstairs are fuckin' real good now and they aren't afraid to share. Jimmy turns up the Wu Tang.
The trigger fish and the tree shrew hump in the night, too 'til the bimbo says,
"I feel like" before each driveling diatribe.

"…and nobody knows sound like me. Nobody knows sound…I hate sound and wear earplugs to work to sleep to everything so I don't have to wear that sound, Man!" said the perturbed technician.

On the chipper side of town, the giggling and tee-heeing is enough to quell thought. Piss drips silently down the thighs of the plebes. Breezes sing through the lips of the leaves.
A broken guitar string heals itself and whispers love into
  a salamander's backside.
The poet likes to think she is piddling her "onomatopoeia" into the porcelain late at night when the neighbors quit cheering on their children with one strop after another.

The muse wants for crisp exactitude.

His hip pops with each step.

The senator is not convinced by the beating of

the hummingbird's wings. Taking a sedative only muffles

life's concert according to the Luddite. Troops stomp

off to war in search of the rat-a-tat-tat of "freedom" and

the squishy blood of the brown people so you don't

have to sell your body to the pimp with the boomin'

system for another gallon of glug glug.

        The bass player wants more vocals in the monitor.

        Wolf Eyes signs with Sub Pop.

The leaf blower shows gumption; but no horse sense;

 Its alarm asks for an answer.

"I've heard about enough of you, Mister!"

The release of the safety leaves only a click. The killer stomps

down a hall in anger.

"...and nobody knows sound like me. Nobody knows

sound...I hate sound and wear earplugs to work to sleep to

everything so I don't have to wear that sound, Man!" said the

perturbed technician.

 There is much fun in the gushing life source;

in a blast to the brains with a blunderbuss;

in a leaf rake across a certain smirk.

The full moon sings its urgency in the minds of the

    night owls.

Later, fenders crunch into each other and a siren screams

its self-importance as the doormen yell, "Laaaaaaaaaaaaaaaaast

Caaaaaaaaaaaaaaaaaaaaaaaaaaaalll!"

Can you hear yourself think?

Where is your inner voice, El Presidente'?
Can you hear that jingle, jangle, jingle?
The hunger pang of a nation set to the bed of you
gargling Satan's jism. Fur shizzle.
 Because there ARE rivers. Because there are breezes.
Because there are trees blowing in those breezes. Nobody
knows sound like sound like you do hound like you do
now.
Like bats and sonar.
A billion boots crunch broken iPods like frozen snow
and skulls of those that have held the nightmares of
these masses.
Brother, can you hear me?
Can you see me near you?
Brother, can you feel me?
Is that you singing?
Eat some pie or shut it!

                              Do you remember
the first time you heard DEVO while John Cage hunted
mushrooms and danced to the twigs' snap?
Remember?

                              Ilsa was thanking
god that farts were audible and munching on corn chips?
Meanwhile, there was an interminable hiss in the PA
and the featured speaker could not be understood as
your stomach grumbled and some chump cracked his
knuckles and sucked on Mentho-Lyptus when he wasn't
hacking up last-night's phlegm.
Schuller sneezes through a sizable schnozz.
Kaufmann pops a cough drop.
The ball continues bouncing against the wall as the
faucet drips and a dwarf in wooden shoes does French-

Press-fueled wind sprints on the wooden floors of your fragile mind.

Time to jet to the Zendo, Fifi.

Their encroachment sometimes welcome, sometimes haunting can send a grown man to the john, the pulpit, the confessional, the madhouse.

The same goes for all beings.

Lhasa Apso yelp. Wolves bay. A car explodes. Little kitty cats mew.

Daddy's got a squeezebox. Mommy cries herself to sleep. Bob saves up for a parabolic microphone with the crumpled cash he makes squeegeeing sedan windows. Frank wears earplugs, though he is deaf. The buzz continues.

The checks come in the mail to pay for the buffering and the AC units drown out the crimes of the night.

Love and happiness conquer the banal screams of youths and during the winter months even Bach and Beethoven are muffled in the roar of the heaters, blowing their suffocating breath to keep the anemic from teeth chatters and shivers.

A well-placed bug captures the ensuing moans but can never take from her the past dalliances of the night and the voices for which she yearns. He'll never say, "I love you." Ashamed of her lisp, he mutters to himself as he backs away each morning, when the sickness is at its most audible. The coffee maker percolates to the ticking of the clock.

The Sawtooth Mountains invite Morricone to the piazza and the nuns beg their pupils to cease.

On the chipper side of town, the giggling and tee-heeing is enough to quell thought. Piss drips silently down the thighs of the plebes. Breezes sing through the lips of the leaves. A broken guitar string heals itself and whispers love into a salamander's backside.

The muse wants for crisp exactitude. The listener is not convinced by the beating of the hummingbird's wings. Karin is crazed by cuckoos in the night.

                              "I've heard about enough
of you, Mister!"
Taking a sedative only parlays a concert according to the Luddite. Troops stomp off to war in search of boom boom and the squishy blood of the brown people so you don't have to sell your iPod.

The release of the safety hardly makes a noise. The killer stomps down a hall in anger.

                              Knees knock.

The full moon sings as Peter turns off the radio and locks the gates.

HUNGER

When puppies run
about in the street
and cars are busy
taking their owners
to their destinations,
soup
is not avoidable.

WHY I CAN'T RUN A THOUSAND MILES
PER HOUR

Funny how I dreamt of tearing
my face from Pompeii stone
last year as the gout
continued its assault on my
agility
a letter opener removed a kidney
from Z
or was it S?
Maybe Q?
In my sleep.

Who can tell when there is this volcano
from your mouth
as my father lost the ability to speak
and my Achilles' don't propel any longer.

Sincerely knowing the abacus was losing track
and fields of daffodils were silk rapture
up a crazed kid at the Dollar Store,
and aliens administered your first pap smear
in years
or some shit.

I'm reaching for a cork
for you to put in it.

No worries, though.
I'm not going to act on my thoughts.

I'll have to retrace my Pepto dismal diary
lick the mud off your corns and hope
for better Casey Stengelese
burps from your mom's
backside.
Does that fit in here?
If it does, I don't know why.
The rookie can't bunt
to save his life
and they call
football
what's done in
domes.

We aimless gophers
crippled by
the time and magazine news
that thought we knew better.

So,
shave with no mirrors.
I'll open the shades
and drink what's in the fridge.
The rest of you can do without me
today.
Tomorrow, you'd better
have your boots on.
I'm gonna run circles around
your skinny little asses
inebriate the meek
and stack cheese like mice architects.
...and tell me this:

Who fucked Mussolini's mom when she
was pregnant with 'im?
Poking him in his fontanel and
then the trains ran on time
with fascism?

Those were the days, huh Bub?

Who shot the shot?
I did!
winning the Harley Race wars
scars on all my victims to be.
I was lauded afterwards for
awarding slaves to all the
paupers
and advancing Prince to his
upper POP status
…and Glockenspiels were invented
amidst the ensuing orgy!!!
But "Who'll" is fun to say too, Seuss.
Like "Who'll we knuckle up tomorrow, Cassius?"
And I free them all with an afternoon
siesta.

Oh never mind!!!

Just lather up your limp dickski
with leather gloves covered in whiskey
and pour another for dear ol' Studs.

If you're working,
dream of suicide.

Me?

I'm about to pop open another.

and sing a song about sandwiches.

...or something about dropping bowling balls

from copters on cloverleaves at

rush hour.

That's a clit-tickler in me funny bone.

Jesus, get your shit together, Kids!

It's the rapture that's comin'.

And if you know what that is

you're an imbecile.

Still, all is forgiven.

It's that kind of day

Though I limp this way.

CONTROL FROM THE HIP

You can't control others, of course,
but you can watch can't control others, of course,
or watch out watch can't control
for them off course.
If someone is shooting off course
can't control from the hip at work
or at home off course control can't,
you've got to take cover from the hip
and wait until they wear themselves out.

Can't control from the hip, of course,
to watch out for them.
If someone is shooting from the hip
at work or at home, of course,
you've got to take cover
and wait until they wear themselves
out at work, off course, of course,
can't control others from the hip.

MINDSHAPING

When a guy is singing about toilet paper,
empty solar and scrapped tractors,
unwanted babies and rotten teeth
like a neuron in our supercluster
especially towards the end
almost every material thing
that was stolen
clears the mind and soul
while you are running errands
that the poor and middle class
depend on in your approach
to listening to learn
more about poster art
that helps shape the minds
of student, jazz artists
it is best to sleep a little longer.
Dream, Baby, Dream.

THE LIAR HAS A SQUIRREL

In my dream, you were walking forward as the mercury
rose in vile and depressing music from a chorus of
unemployed frogs.

The woods smelled like mildew and fresh-dropped dung.
You attempted to escape, but could not.
I leapt forward.
Circumstances worsened with confused sweat bees.
You were terrified and thirsty for dust.
My mind yelled out the word "Hellziburton" when the
floor morphed into a lake.
The birdsongs each tuned an octave higher but muted
and slowed… standing ankle deep in whatever that
reflected the horse-faced attendants...the church bell rang.
I dreamt that we were not a monster, but rather a wise,
old rain barrel
loathing the fact that we had to listen at all.
Rain, we wanted, not words.

"Words!???

Tears, blood and rain can't be bothered with words!
and we were there to wash all the faces, toes sinking into
the black clouds
damp from morning dew.
Tickling a sharp cheddar with tiny strobes in a villa called
No Bread.
Mustard filled their veins.
Bratwursts turned to fear and plotted war.

In my dream, I felt laughter sirens calling my name.
I told your girlfriend to continue shopping and next thing
I'm in a room with a lot of grape popsicles on top of me.
I was not sure if I approved of the left turn at Wigslop
and the horny Leprechaun peeking out
from behind a tree whispering
"Mmm. Sticky. Mmm. Sticky."
I dreamt that I don't recall flowers.
He didn't have any.
She didn't have any.
In my dreams, I asked him why he never left me and he said
cuz he doesn't have any.
She didn't have any.
But I knew he was lying
and that he had a squirrel now.

DREAMING STREET SIGNS

No dreaming dogs on school property

No dreaming on the grass

No dreaming first Tuesday of the month, Noon to 3 p.m.

No dreaming this side of street

Dream Stop

Caution! Slow Dreaming

Caution! Children Dreaming

Caution! Deer Dreaming

Caution! Pavement is Slippery When Dreaming

FUCKING STREET SIGNS

No fucking dogs on school property
No fucking on the grass
No fucking first Tuesday of the month, Noon to 3 p.m.
No fucking this side of street
Fuck Stop
Caution! Slow Fucking
Caution! Children Fucking
Caution! Deer Fucking
Caution! Pavement is Slippery When Fucking

ON YOUR ODDER

To draw on your odder resources
feel free to move now I forgot to remember
its pudding or custard or what I forgot to remember
a dream a dream a dad a mom I forgot to remember
and you may need to surprise a few people
with some crazy moves, yourself, Buster!

Your secrets are still safe,
or at least most of them
are, so feel free to move ahead.

Chew on your odder reports
to surprise a few crazy moves.
Your secrets are free: move ahead.
Dream of packaging sweet potatoes
and carrots near a rather large mirror.
Every other time you look to the right,
the reflection is him: Dad.
You're wearing his sweater.
The tubers are covered in dust.
The autumnal breeze rustles the hanging
petroleum sacks behind
and over your left shoulder
(the path to glory; the disappointment; soon to be broken)
fucking with the fight or flight instinct.
Warmin' up. Layers off.
Rockin' a Bob Reuter tee shirt
and the Mother Hen is sweeping leaves up the ramp
and out the door into the parking lot.

"In the spring, I'll be sweeping up blossoms," she said.
Dream, Baby, Dream. Wake up laughing at the wrong
   time of night.
Wake up terrified before a day of work weighing on
   your mind, body and soul.
Take it from a closeted prima donna, and fork over
   the cash, Chump.

Open up to new people:
friends,
clients,
idiots,
unemployed shortstops,
folks on the street,
your fucking neighbor.

Get gregarious?
Back slide to the side is out
in force now.
Convert them to your cause.
Don't give up!

DO SOME SQUATS

Stop in the mountains praying
surroundings, reflection
your smoking cures salmon
sexy, mid-day names
died of meningitis.

They thought it was a game.

Do not recall
secret messages transmitting
in the wrong word
between trees
blaming me.
Stop it shit twit that invites
a pause to do some squats,
to wander and soak
people on the same page
can suffocate new ideas
urban, often set in squalid
surroundings, reflecting
the Great Depression
as well as German expressionism's
ex.

…and those dumb Pollack jokes
turned to blonde pokes…
Gimme the fucking punch line
and let's watch Sugar Ray and
Ali splash the paint.

They thought it was a game.
Not the fighters! Idiot!

Did you even read this?

AT LEAST QUESTION

Lose to a breakthrough
mentally, not quite there.
Pushing and shit
will come.
Don't try.
Give up.

To don't know, try.
Today's energy is question time
perfect for philosophizing,
the harder time play
expect the epiphany
know why to come quietly
quite yet don't know authority
why, but having
a harder question time possible
dealing with you don't know today.
Try to you harder level
the playing field authority
you don't know why,
but you're having a harder
time dealing with today
level playing.

Try to don't know
you're level playing field
if question possible,
or at least question of don't
know why the rules of play

if possible, or at least question
the rules of harder time play
but you don't know why
with authority today.

WASTE CAPITAL

Crisscrossing lanes chuckin'
Goodwill croquet balls off the bridge
to disappointment on those days
when you really want to hire
a transportation engineer to get to the heart of the issue
— but you never seem to quite make it—
doesn't mean the day is a waste
(capital money could be allocated),
because all this thought is sure
to yield good ideas.

NO MOPPING THE COSMIC SLOP

Yeah, Big Boy.
That ferocious wheel ride
put you over the top.
The music and all
took a flight beyond
means: Observing a daughter shoplift,
large amounts of junk food by the pound
out with this 40-year old dude
who can do Venmo, or PayPal, under duress?

Relocated to the mermaid
watercolors on paper, so make art,
confuse strangers (huge swanky party)
exposure to Roundup Weed swallowed
years: the opposite of dating
which spilled outside
why I'm so amped it does pair well.

I hit BOOM. It ejected us.
gRIMaced meAd. Crammed Age.
Graced Mime. You know.
The usual.
You wonder where everything is
and then you find it
in a glass of pizazz!

No smoking the cosmic slop;
no random asteroid buggery;
no false gods after dark;

no monotheistic nincompoopery
out of orbit...

I forget the rest.

Like Reagan and that puked pea soup
that jellybean drip drop economic droop.
Mondaize on the way, when we miss
the supermoon the stars and miss
the discussion at bars with the teeveez on.

March on the pavement to the un-reality dork.
Sip on the other end of your gun sight
end of your rights.

Get the better (of an adversary or competitor,
for example)
by using a crucial, often hidden resource.
Thailand is a guitarlike cooking,
playing music, dancing or drawing.
After the fast-moving dance full of frolicking
footwork putting it at risk for health,
nuts seem like a mixed bag for two
bills introduced at the beginning of October
from fatty acids found in fish,
but nuts have them too.

No cover charge and the flies are always cold.

RUBBLE

When a certain level of oomph
has gone from the jets
you put the junk in the hangar.
Huh?
But NOW airing the lungs past
the Dutchtown corner store the ladies
have spied my sneakers
and comment as I nod and smirk,
not sure what what what?

Up the front porch steps and cracking up
as the key turns.
A rambling, stumbling and tumbling toddler
is amused that a dog is shitting on the sidewalk
across the way.
The kid jabbers and sings of the wonder of defecation
running ahead of the crowd.
"Poop Poop Poop Poop Poop Poop Poop!"

The weather is good for the lazy ambling.
Life is life.
A pebble or seed is lodged in the craw.
Get your oyster, yuppie and woohooo warriors.
It is your Saturday as the bombs drop...
and now it is time to step inside
for the matrons are perturbed.
Their perceived order has been upset once again
and the world topples into rubble,
both physical and mental.

NOT THE FINAL SNAFU

Tools that change the way people think
can be loves to stop now.
We compiled reflections on the life.
These are indications.
You can deal with any crazy tissue
that pops up today buttchoo
half believe in yourself!
Things are better than you realize
even if this snafu looks like the end
of the world.
There is always time to drop
water balloons on the Gendarmerie,
chortling all the while in a time
of surprises and disguises.

STRESS LESS (or a lightness of vision)

The almost.
I've got it.
The almost will take the
game most nights.
I'll have another
then wish I was some-
where someone else.
No slaphappy ding-a-ling.
It's inevitable.
I know it.
Still,
there's no one to
stop it.
No mopeydope can.
It is hope which tosses
such feelings aside.
Only hope.
We must hope for a better
tomorrow as
human beings...or else.
Or else what?
One will say,
"Hope is a crutch."
Hope is an anomaly.
Hope for less ennui.
Hope is punk as fuck?
Then why?
If why,
then how?

An epiphany:
Stress kills.
So don't worry.
Stop watching as much.
Listen and act.
That is it.

SYMPTOM #1

Fear wrote the book.
Had it published.
Did promotional.
Ignorance did legwork.
Swallowed it.
Wore for a wrap.
As love flew last birdsy
look see.
Choking on life's pesticide,
Daddy likes children.

Poison invites poison.
Cancer throws party.
All cumwallowing in noise.
Mickey Mouse gives a reach around.

See average.
Going about day
blowing leaves.
Not content
that breeze
would do it
more peacefully.
That will kill.
Be the death of leisure.
The deconomics of introspection.

Business
Confuses spirit.

Everyday confusion
Lathers dead souls...
Keeps remote control sales up.
Put faith in lazy ballot system.
Three-hour commute and
Microwaved dinner.
Feed dog horse
Melt together.

Yummy churchstate toast!
Mmmmmm!

Idea
Drowned in task
Dig grave, Lover.
Scratch at the lid
of coffin.
Scrape
Dust into gasping lungs

Mommy?

***

There's brilliance:
a blazing inferno.
Set
gathering to see end.
Enamored with results
too lazy to ask why.
Seek easy answer.
Sleeping.

Dream of brighter tomesterday.
Happy sorrow yesmorrow mustard gas
blossoms and wafts sweetly.
Clickle tit
tickle clit
smile child
while spitting.
Pay to swallow

A most fascinating subject
still a glimmering
hope, a fuzzed-out
light,
a muted and distorted signal

Sure answer there.
Sit distracted.
Eat popcorn cheese whiz.
Pray first down…
Capture villain…
Release hostage…
Prayers be heard
from damsel with nice onions
answered in multi-vitamins.

Fear evil
but promote.
Swallow facsimile.
Sprinkle granulated nothing
on false hope regurgitates.
Building idols of illusion
scorning the

visionaries
who step aside.

Asking forgiveness.
Strangling, squeezing
last bones in
white gloves clenched
whores open minds
and there are always happy endings.

Daddy likes feculence.
Makes deal.
Snorkels with lemmings

LATE NIGHT RADIO

You've all heard the stories:
There are drunken marauders storming the station late at
night. They put a gun to the DJ's head and demand Air
Supply—any Air Supply—at 45 revolutions per minute.
Then the jock spewing through a smirk "Don't ever utter
revolution and air supply in the same sentence again,
Shitbird. We can conquer the world without breathing!"

Or, the one about the man with a half-shattered mind,
alone in a room with a microphone, two turntables
and a cassette player, digging through a box of cassette
tapes and mumbling into a live microphone about that
perfect track, wishing it was on his fingertips, wishing it
were on the air, wishing for anything but this moment
which yawns with ennui in the ears of some listeners and
fascinates others who revel in the absurd—all unaware
that a pizza delivery girl enters the room on a skateboard,
strips, squats up on an office chair and spins with mad
abandon whilst lustfully lapping up music from dusty
LPs, her hands turning the records clockwise across her
tongue so that she ingests so much E Minor tragedy
that she begins to weep. Not long after, the host lays his
fingers on that Charley Pride he was searching for and the
girl dissolves into dust, tears and all...

Then there's the story you like to tell about how you heard
this late-night jock babbling at a bar about some older
woman who called claiming she used to talk to Moondog
on the bus as they rode through the Lower East Side back

in the 70's...or was it the 60's...and something about him
having attended the Missouri School for the Blind and it
was kind of weird because he, himself, the radio guy, was
riding the 13 to the Central West End, reading DeLillo
when he heard the woman's voice. She was climbing into
the bus with a walker and he watched her and listened
to her conversation with the bus driver and she got
off at Barnes to work at a gift shop...and no, he didn't
introduce himself.

Or, the federal judge crying on the phone to the host
because he was rude and hung up on him while he was
forlorn and riding around the East Side and just wanted
to hear some Tull while he and a transvestite ate jet pops
in the back of a limo.

None of it is true though. They are all urban legend
or lies! None of that could ever happen on late-night
radio to late-night radio hosts. For events such as those
to occur, for instance, at KDHX at 1:45 on a Friday
morning, the sun would have to implode and Reagan
would reincarnate as son of John Denver to save the
world from schmaltz. Yes, for such arrangements to
be made, that much would be imperative, you innocent
clams who yearn to produce such pearls.

No, what happens at KDHX during late-night radio is
beyond words. I couldn't describe it even if I remembered
any of it. It is as if aliens steal my memory as I exit the
building after hosting an episode of The No Show and I
am left to float home on a beam of light in a fringe-top
horseless carriage.

I mean I have the recordings to prove to myself that I was at the station, the overhauled bakery on Magnolia. That's me on the recordings. The crumpled playlists are there in my bag and archived on the station's website.

I recall standing outside the station smoking a quick cig as some kids swerved through an intersection after carjacking a fraught damsel chasing down the street with cell phone to head, blood trickling down her torn hose and left knee. And last summer, I stopped by the station on my bicycle to check my email and found two punk-rock show producers outside talking to the police about the woman who was handcuffed in the backseat of the squad car. She had stopped her truck while one of them was loading records into his. She ran towards him screaming, "I can't stand it anymore!" and nothing else.

However, these incidents all happened outside the station.

Most nights when I'm not doing the show and have stopped by to listen to something or do some audio work on the computer in Studio A or B, Bob Reuter, Kevin Lawrence or another off-air DJ will be there doing the same thing or finishing some correspondence. I have a perfect recollection of those nights...and each Thursday as I enter the studio and Josh Weinstein is riveting the heads of his listeners to the heavens, I am fully aware and embarrassed to be sharing the same call letters.

But my friends claim they have visited me while I was doing the show and left because I wouldn't talk to or even look at them and the phone would ring and I'd quote what sounded like Zorn's horn and Bukowski mixed together and slam the phone down, cackling and frothing at the mouth while grabbing an LP with my other hand and smashing it across the console. But you can't trust those loons; they feed buffalo chips to starving Sioux and argue over soda products and colors of caulk. I can only hope that they, too, will someday learn what it is like, "to be in the zone."

I can only share one late-night KDHX story with you and hope that it resembles the story I would tell if I could remember anything about doing my show because it happened before midnight on New Year's Eve a couple years back and so was not yet in my sense of time, late night.

I was covering another host's show, so he could hold one of his underground cheese-curls and sparkling water orgies. The previous host had left in a huff, shrieking something about hippies or long-hairs or something, as I spun into the program with some old Pere Ubu and was having a leisurely go of it, like most veteran hosts do when the phone calls aren't rapid fire and the tracks are long enough to type in a playlist allowing mind and fingers to cue up the next track, PSA or the like. I answered a couple of requests for material which I could not fill. No sweat. I didn't have the material. It was not my show. "Enjoy the bubbly, sweet birdies-of-the-night. I'm a grinning volunteer, bridled only by insouciance and a need for solitude huddled in a small room with my fingers at the controls of the airwaves and a live internet stream fueled by nameless urges and caffeine," I said to the clock.

Later, I recalled my wish to spend a New Year's Eve on my back atop a hill or mountain, cocooned in a thermal sleeping bag with a view of the stars and planets. I was spinning records and imagining such a night when I came across "I Am God" from Negativland's 1993 album "Free." It is a reflective, sometimes shocking and humorous audio collage which opens with children singing about the ecumenical movement and features a repeated chant of "I am God. You are God. We are all God." Surely a piece which might incite a response; people being so trigger happy when it comes to their religious beliefs, I thought.

I mean, I've heard the stories about radio personalities being shot in the parking lot outside other radio stations and I've heard other producers tell stories about being threatened by nutbag callers. I have only recently been brave enough to watch Play Misty for Me so I fathomed that I might draw some frustrated demon out of the cold, dark night.
Nope. Wrong.
Didn't have a call for the rest of the show.

I had a couple bands and a party to catch afterward, so I was packed up and ready to roll when I podded up the announcement at the end of the show and cleared the way for the next show's hosts. I shouldered my bag of tricks and walked outside with my attention focused on the upcoming hours.

I had ambled about halfway down Magnolia to Grand when the fireworks and gunfire announced midnight on the South Side. There were a couple kids across the street launching bottle rockets willy-nilly in all directions and I thought for a moment that I might make a likely target, but rounded the Montessori on the corner and walked up Grand free of damage. The gunfire sounded automatically, clearly and rapidly, but distantly.

I was home, re-garbed, ready for action, back out the door and by 12:20, I had parked the car halfway between the bars and the house party and was standing in CBGB with an Oatmeal Stout and a Gambrinus-like thirst. A Jan Primus' spirit sang softly in a drunken woman's ear as he shot me a wink fueled with jiggers of corn. Her squirming disgust was pitiful. Like souls sleeping dreamlessly, like cyborgs on Soma, she was having none of it. There was still a hint of displeasure to show for her pride, though, so I wrestled the spirit away and we shared old memories from having been at play between our respective headphones and four walls.

DUSK AT THE WHISKEY BAR

Awaiting the yogi and a cleansing cloud of smoke.
In ten minutes, no one will remember this.
Look around.
Death and sore tits blow in around the door
and window frames, but the dingbats
meet it with hot air, a collective chortle
and a rehashing of falsities.

Victory is anyone's guess.
The scorecards are a mess at this point
since the tweaker pinch ran for the ogre.
A taxi runs a red. On a dirty plate,
in the bottom half of the eighth,
grenades tossed from the street food stands
taste like pineapple. No need for a fork.

Snipers have the skulls in their sights.
They're ready to strike
with every fourth ball.
The dorks do the wave
and the umpires fart in the breeze.
The medicine men are buried in popcorn
as the cavalry approaches
to rub out the village.
All intelligence is run through a universe
where a fly sits atop a water drop
on the next table.
In ten minutes, nobody will remember

POST DRINKS

Driving home in the Midnight zone
don't make much sense
cause it's snowing

nearly subzero temps
listening to Finn's Motel
coming over me

no slick streets yet
got some new treads
and the bills are paid

the henna topped bartender
sent me home
in fine shape.

WHAT'S MAGIC CAKE?

There is a strange forgetfulness of god
without making a big fuss with her raw vulnerability.
                    The sinking helicopters were linked
to the food cleaning the upstairs.

Find it immensely satisfying when she announces, in typical,
soft-spoken Latin,
                    "the basal tear, the emotional tear and
the reflex tear."
 But she said that claim was far from the truth approached
on jet skis
            nestled at the curve
 used to be an income stream.

                    Like a beacon to like-minded souls,
reading your mind like Hector B. Poole, blessed by a
terrifying,
                    wind-whipped wildfire, willfully
ignore medical science.
            MILF traded punches after a debate then crept
gingerly into reclining chairs
and rushed to the attic, pulling the folding stairs up.

                    In Rome, bears could possibly
be dealing with flash freezing fluff turned into a pile of
charred and twisted debris.
The big E apologized and took a leave of absence stuck
permanently

in their towering beehive bouffant gather-by-the-river hairdo, said the Pope.

"Everything voodoo can do can can do better", she said, gently rubbing her vageen.

REPLACING OIL, HATE AND LIGHTNING STRIKES

What cow jumped the moon? Dear swift horn, dear
wept tear near grass herds on wind and that notion of
feces in your olfactory memory. That got you down?
You promised to report.
You, the best reporter.
I forgive you and your impotent pen
and your scabbed over inkwell.

You never did, I know, but it's fun to pretend
in that whatever wind of bovine stench, that ha ha ha.
Imagine that it didn't happen and she was still chuckling.
Oh! The joy. Imagine if sand was the sea.

Oh! We would have more glass.
Cheap glass.
Glass to break.
Glass to eat.
Glass to chug.
Glass to belch in shards.

Through bleeding lips and chipped teeth we
would learn to enjoy it.
Even to digest it.
Like we did oil and hate and genital
friction amidst thunderstorms and the
limitless spending at box stores
with lightning bolt scars on our haunches.
Now I want that report even more.

Bay at the moon, for me.
Get wolfy. Micturate in the weed.
Piss your love in the breeze.
Take me to your cave walls.
Where you explain it all.

KIDS A PEEK

The political guru board game
with everyone dancing to Marvin Gaye
is as lush and atmospheric as any Gothic horror
and want to go fast go is not personal, permanent,
or perfect.
Inventive works that disassemble meaning
COSTUME KIDS is just complete thumbing
of the nose to be miserable in your own goodness.
GIVE YOUR KIDS A PEEK
INSIDE THE PRESIDENCY
aka Dr. Cumfizzles jolly romp.
In a wider sense, the cumming legal duel:
legs up in the air, but tossed salad expectations
are reduced to zero.

A LITTLE SCRATCHY

I don't know what
you're having for breakfast,
but howza 'bout this?

Imagine a masturbation scene
in a Tarantino flick.
Maybe Lynch?
Is it Dean Stockwell?
Is it him?

Would have to be
someone of his ilk.
He is naked and watching
WHEEL OF FORTUNE
with the sound off.

He's got his record player goin'
and it is a dark night.
He had five or ten too many.
Toes curl in shag carpet.

"Everything is Beautiful"
by Ray Stephens
is now getting laid
by the needle.

For the record,
It's a little scratchy.

FOR THE GOOD WILL

Did someone say can of peas? or t.p.?
The survival clan that wipes the asses
feeds the masses,
but shit don't make no sense.

Wait what? I am confused.
Was it P.? or C.?
Covid mental confusion
or the drugs
or the mugs standing on the street
begging for money?
or the Hugs we crave

In the land of the brave
the dying
the sighing
Freedom
and the lack thereof?
The salute to a hand shake
lost the elbow grease.

How do you do?
I am confused.
The shelter lost to Helter Skelter
the land of the cross?
No region here folks
The land of the tokes
The tokes and the currency
The land of the salt?

Assault or pepper spray?
I think I want both?
A good struggle?
Is that what they mean?

Oh, that's right
the higher power has taken
my rights and soul
to control the sewn pockets
from a pair of pants
for the good will.

Ha!
"Will"
.... oops... did I spill my drink?
Nab that, dab that
Create
all of that.

Your Nazi Nissan
is on the fritz
and there is a streak
of orange sherbet
in the evening sky.

Drink up folks, and enjoy the show.

FILETED BRONTOSAURUS AND SARDINES

Make a sandwich for a tornado.
A dizzying array shot
with a camera
by the expeditor
sustained assaults
aimed towards poetry
penguin bagpipes
who don't know
the secrets of the albino
that you have to crank
until wildest Brazilian
amidst a soapwax opera
were a little bit timid
still not divorced
from journalism
frozen to the sidewalk of failure.
They're usually green and slightly sweet.
They're called nuts.
Fruit and nuts
on Werner's salad?
Who tossed it?

People had objections
in livid vain blood clots
do very, very strange rituals
and it's relentless
self-inspection.
She said, "Words
parody your shadow."

He: "I'm too short."
She: "Try it with some magazines."

Albatross then.
On marbled rye
fileted Brontosaurus
sliced oh so thin
with some diced sardines.
Did you get enough
to eat, Honey?

Flap to escape
the horizon
and kiss the moon.
When there whip
kelp instead of kale
dressing on the side
payments hush hush.

One way or another
the bastards stiff her.
Everyone knows
its windy.

Go head deny
the peanut butter cock
advertisement.
I seent it!

Missy said blerp,
but she believes
in ART

from the balcony.

Memories
Fireworks
Puff
Puff

2020 fucked you
and left $600 on the bedside table.

2021 is all yours.
Put it in a blender and make magic.
Belch&Felchslap reality, Folks!
Abort memory.
Nostalgia is for creeps!
It is time to make a new world.
Do as I said, not as I did.

GUSH

In between the highlight films and kitty videos
there is blood in the stool of your make up.
See it swirling down the bowl as you
stand up and turn to look down
or miss it as you check your look in the mirror.
In South America it swirls one way.
In Mongolia it swirls the other.
Clock tick counter Glock click
licks the sand of the time of your is
was
might have been
away.
Name the difference. Draw the line.
Fear and ignorance makes some tasty
Hate.
Talking to one another doesn't change the fact;
EVIDENTLY.
nor does your method
Your horsepower
Your wealth
Your flipped bird in traffic urgency
The clack of cuffs
The fence
The signs
The cold shoulder
It is in the pipes.

It is in the sewers.

It is dripping from the cave walls.

It is amidst the sunshine.

In the veins.

The arteries.

The moon and the sun and you are made

from the same.

Slop.

The same plants that

make your flags.

Your Styrofoam.

Your sandals

YOUR FLIP FLOPS

and

THONGS.

Your Sunday Funday.

Your happy pills.

Your goofballs and elixirs.

Your slow drip plastic fork drive thru convenience.

It has soaked into the soil where

your heroes dance in victory

in celebration of one goal over another

or another click bait enticement and

excitement.

It lubricates the rocks

and gives your neighbor

Ebola.

Victories of nothingness are

celebrated by useless whores

and cubicle slaves
upon the dead.
As you fix your hair while looking in the mirror.
AND ANOTHER GUN SHOT
makes it drip and gush.
It is in the streets
outside the bodega.

Don't taste it.
Don't look.
The strategies of the genius always win
while you check your bank account.
While you discuss salad and colors of caulk,
the Colonel rapes the maid after
she dusts and shines.

SWARM

You can sweat the victory
of the wage slaves'
fear of the terror in the leaves.
The anxiety over toast
has a spot in your coffee klatch
cluck cluck and apoplectic sputtering
about the color of caulk.
Crumbs in office and between
your heaving breasts has you
weeping for more comfort in your
ass-whipping material and this
and that.
But...
Is it other people that make you?
Birds?
Bugs?
The wind?
Take it among the rituals
the nonsense swarm of the crowds
the suckling of glass teats even...
Maybe not? I know, but do you?
Or the nonsensical babble in a brook
and in that same crowd, to continue.
"I like to hear you talk about the things you
have to say."
What? Why?
This and that and failure is a difficult meal
to swallow on a tired phone
with a jelly donut.

ONLY CANNIBALS TAKE HEART

Perhaps I should take heart
that you even speak to yourself
in that seldom-viewed blog
that I can't seem to find
on mornings when I search
for such nothings,
but only cannibals take heart.

Prescribe downtime and contemplation
to figure out this mess and sweep
the bunnies from their corners,
but I like their crunchiness
on the souls of my bare feet
and downtime is not about sweeping.

Were I to walk to the answer,
it would only take a month.
I would find you in a dozen faces.
I would find us in trouble again.
I could do it only to distance myself
from whatever future they say there is...
or I could do it for focus.

The capitalists say I have four days
free of extraneous cash and work
to cypher it out.

I shoot you as you shoot me,
but we don't recognize
the barbs.

Why just this morning, I thought it
was just another ache or pain.
Rolled over and groaned, nearly
breaking my schwanzstucker off
in the process.

Only then did I remember that
I was dreaming about running after
you, west on Magnolia to Kingshighway
and east to Sauget.

THE GIVE AND GO

Did you know?
The expeditor was talking to the gumbo
and wouldn't listen to the wisdom
of the andouille when dialysis landed
on the fish ballot.

The chuckleheads took it
as a clue to ignore.
Given their dos and don'ts;
Their will and wont's
and what comes with the donuts
and coffee, they had to question
the regularity of the clouds' offerings.

The diners were oblivious
as the osprey with the arrow in its throat cried.

The give and go.
You came and you went.
You go along. You get along.
But sometimes,
you gotta exclaim,
"What?!!!"

BIRD SHIT

For what does the impotent songbird sing?
(or does it?)
For one chance at immortality?
For the hope that one of his tunes,
his riffs
will stick in the sap
of a horny maple tree?
Or in the ear of a jazz man?
Or perhaps he is only attempting to
torture the insomniacs
who lie awake from nightmares
of DDT
before the wings go twitching and then
stiff
before the death rattle hits
after
Tweet, Tweet, Tweedily Deet
and the song ends in one final percussion
Feathers and bone on sidewalk
or sunbaked ground
and the radio clicks on for no one to hear
or you trying to plug the
USB cord into its ass
so you can download it
to your iPod or some such.

What if said bird took a flamingo-like stance
and grasped pen with its foot?
Penned a cease-and-desist order
to god and man
before crapping on leaves and twigs?

Would that make him or her more-or-less an artist?
More?
Less?

What say you, academic credit boy?
If birdy pays his tuition
Is it worth a listen?
Crap and all?

DREAD OF NIGHT

Is this Hell?
Life is limbo. A bit worse than Hell.
Depending on one's appetite
for the unknown.

How much time is there
to endure the sands?
To dread the wonder of my graying
hair?
To walk to the edge of the waves?
To ponder volatile lips of
an insane person?
To endow pockets with sweetness?
To make sleep possible to porcupines?

Or a poem about the burning of
yachts at a convention with no
traffic light we should've stopped
at long ago for a sandwich.

No. Remind the phallus of all its lies.
Kiss the stars.
Forgive us.
Forget us.
Let us forgive us.
The sins of the father. Endless war.
The president of slavery and
the rashes on the wrists of the
dishwashers.

Never forgetting that this
is as shallow as the mallow of a
dog's bone.

Yet there is the promise of tomorrow's
Sun.

WHY I WON'T GO ON SAFARI WITH YOU

I mean, I like the outdoors and a free trip to the
Congo seems cool and all. I even enjoy, in a masochistic
way, getting dust in my eyes and losing weight from
water-borne diseases.

I surely can't imagine murdering a giraffe and lying down
next to its majestic neck for a selfie or
riding around in a jeep with your coked-up friends
armed with guns they know little about.

That makes me nervous, but hey,
a party's a party…
and it's not that I imagine hunting wild animals in their
    natural
habitat might make me as suicidal as Hemingway on a
Jack Daniels bender…even if I was only along for the ride.

No, none of those reasons really lead me not to join
    you on safari.

In the end, it's not even that you say tomato and I say
    tomato.

Or that you treat your employees like shit.

Or that your sandwiches are sub-par bleh fit for only the
    most-stoned frat boy.

No, the reason I won't go on safari with you is that I say
    potato and you say clitorectomy.

WAGESLAVE ALGEBRA

Think of your favorite memories
of Tommy Chong and you're AT THE PLACE
and he says something like,
"Hey, Man. You keep peelin'
that book, Man."

It's Bukowski, Tommy. It's Bukowski.
If it wasn't for Carver or a surprise Angel
in the night, I wouldn't have made it.

"All right, Man, but you had that far out
look, Man."

Yeah. Thanks for noticing.

But, let's play with words.

For instance::::?

Sow. Sow? So. Sew?

Ugh.

Fuck idiot wage slave mumble survival
no-one ever retains these Idiots.
How aggressive are the flippers getting?
Who asks, "What Fun part about the asteroid?"
Some genius is going to have to corral the fire tornado!

So we started:
Lick it and stick it on top
of the crack when you have joint
drama meanwhile rejecting butt makeup
Fun part about the asteroid
Fun part about the asteroid.

Roots return to innocence lost
I rode my hangover buzz
and tossed through digital mania.

Meet each moment without clinging.

THERE IS NO FARTHER

without FART
in your flip flops and dolphins
make horrible bus boys.
(Is there an echo in here?)
Use dummy gladhands when air lines
are disconnected and put an 'x'
after those you leave.

They told you to cum,
but you were already there,
you Big Silly.

My ears are ringing.
Someone is thinking of me.
Give me SOMETHING, Millionaire Janitor!
It's weird when people seek pleasure
and beautiful, functional, suitable coffin
spacepain translated in Google
and a cherished Cockatoo, Lopglop bingbop,
and friends massing on the jungle gym.

I'm down for affliction.
Able to help with mental yoga
and flossing.
Real good at being a gofer
and smashing your televisionminds.

Die because the droolers get in the way
with they're puritanical viscosity
and wormtrooper response dribble.

Deep breaths.
Ah.

The time to something
is sometime do anything
any time or do something
sometime.

There is a couple
like a dumpster fire
across the street
A dumpster fire with hand
grenades never
What? Do they sell explosives
at THE DOLLAR STORE!!!?

An absurdly early admonition acknowledges
the smell of South Grand in the morning
and she felt the scorn of the cashier when
she walked in right after the delivery guy
who looked like he was coming to pick up
an amp he left behind "last night."
He gave her a look.
She didn't see it
and was wearing a THROW RAG
shirt.
Funny.

She jumped the gun.
The door was open before "opening" time.
Soon there were red shirts upon her as she chose
vegetables and she assured them with a smile
and an evil, red eye.

Getting the looks this early,
like she used to throw at those stepping
outside the lines in the club, seemed comforting.

Now, all she was doing was picking up
and dropping off some goods to a friend
who was hiding away from the Rona.
Didn't give a fuck that there is no time
or had to walk a gauntlet of stares.
The mission is the mission.

SPEW

More energetic and delirious than I'd been in a while,
a customer at the bar upped the giddy with silly shit
spurting forth with innocent excitement about the world
of the new.

"I'm not kidding, Violet," he said to the bartendress.

"I don't care what it is, but I like to try anything I haven't
had before."
"That was good!" he said of a Huber lager. "What else
you got!"
She poured him an American Pale Ale and he piped up
again.

Heads turned.

We were sipping coffee on a day that hadn't quite yet
kick-started itself.

I barely got some lunch in me and was starting to long
for the smoke I had left in my flat.
The coffee bent nothingness into something but
nothing and I felt conscious for the first time since the
whiskey and chronic buzz I had put on a couple nights
ago, before cold and dark days of reading and sleeping.

"I discovered Pizza Hut all-you-can-eat," the wackadoo
continued, loud enough for all in the dining room to
hear.

"Man, I had salad and nine pieces of pizza. And then! I had some cottage cheese and some pudding!"

The cat next to me was now crying into his sleeve, trying his best not to laugh out loud.

"Then! My buddy called and wanted me to hang some dry wall with him! Aaaahhh no, I'm immobilized!"

The shit satellite radio poured more 80s schlock into the mix. I knew I couldn't last long thinking about all the hopeless love I had spent while listening to this dreck but somehow it felt good, sparked by the coffee and an increasing need for inhalation.

"You show me an all-you-can-eat graze bar and I'm there!" he cackled now. "I wish they had a place that had it all. I'd munch cheeseburgers, souvlaki and kani maki!"

This little dude must have a tapeworm, I thought…and how does he know about sushi? He didn't look the type: a buzz cut, weathered face and work-a-day demeanor. But there was something crazy and angelic about him. He took his days with him, I guess. I don't know. I remember thinking that NOW was enough for him and he was definitely enough for all of us. He had us by the ovaries and gonads.

He let us dive down and sink into our own comments about Morrissey and the shit Brit DJ. Let us look out the windows onto the banking public on Grand Boulevard.

Let us sip and wonder "what next?"
And then, "I started drinking when I was five."
Skulls on necks spun, they did.
"I used to sit on my Granddaddy's lap and drink beer,
    Violet."
He had us on the hook again and was reeling us back
in, but I was glad that I was not him, yet jealous and
envious, somehow.

"He used to give me whiskey, too! Ha Ha Ha Ha Ha Ha
    Ha Ha Ha Ha!"

Violet kept herself together somehow. The rest of us
were either stunned or crumbling to pieces, but she was
clocked in and simply grinning a little.

"Do you like that APA? That's what I drink," she said.

I liked her composure, but I wanted more.
"Ah, Man! This is fucking great! What is this????!!"
Violet pointed at the APA tap handle.
"It's kind of fruity!!" he squeaked as the boy to my left
lost it, spewing mucous across his plate of partially eaten
chicken wings.

We all shuffled awkwardly in our spaces. I took another
sip of java and looked back out the glass onto South
Grand. Violet made like she had something urgent to do
in the kitchen.

MUTED WISDOM

In the pre-dawn morning
the call of the birds enraged him.
He rolled out of the hammock
and put his foot in his back pocket.
fell face first into the stars
that contained last night's fire.
The bug bites were portals from the wild
to gather signs, messages, signals and wisdom
from the wind, the critters, the creepy crawlies
and the unheard: those shut out of the media
and board meetings.

Some of the cries of the night are muted,
but the helicopters have eyes...
and there is blood seeping into the roots.
Ants are there to gather and interpret intel.
The same willful ignorance that ignores
the medicine men puts their antennae
music on mute.

MOMENTARY BLASTING

Due to the effects of the value
of being a bilingual real estate agent,
largely ditch them to safety on your concrete
and asphalt projects for a LOT of classical,
opera and folk records on vinyl.
Complete with surprise pyrotechnics
and momentary blasting just to keep you "awake."
Like, NOW.
A bold and versatile Season and Famine
to send the country back, but if it means something
for sudden breathing problems, please let me know!

AMIDST IT ALL

While the waitresses worry about chem trails,
the tine punctures the yolk.
The oxen fire off salvos.
The surgeon butcher's a joke.
The nurses snort the last of the blow.
The Malamute barks at the skunk.
The busboy is suffering grief and sore feet.
The priest is discovering Punk.
The clouds are a fluttering after thought,
though daily, they blot out the sun.
The dirt drinks the rain and the blood of
the masses
and you think you're the only one.

Come trade me your woes for a job full of blows
and a dozen obsequious morons.
I'll smile at your face, let you win the race
and scoff at your enemy pawns.

IN A WORLD WITHOUT BROOMS

When you think it is a perfect day: A watermelon
breakfast, two short walks to nothing, really, followed
by a nap or two and some saffron rice, a ballgame
on the radio, slow, quiet time in the library and maybe
even some slow, sad hugs and kisses with the woman
that drives you towards dreams of HELL YEAH!
and universal know what's out there is in there.

To wake to the smell of tar—like dinosaurs fucking
in their last gasp of hope—sweat-soaked and lonely men
leering at every passing car and the inhabitant of that car
before they lug another roll of tar paper up incline,
near the ladder, nothing gained, but another task done
and the scars to prove it...

Nightmarenoise—the landlady jokes about putting
some more lusty hippos upstairs—the perfection
of the imperfect city making feeble attempts to right itself;
the man that has forgotten about the broom; the 8 a.m.
lawnmower; the meth-blown, but cheap tuck-pointing
crew...and somehow the fan...the white noise drowns
it all out for 20 minutes and makes your dick and nipples
hard and you have that dream again as you drift off
on a day off even when the sheets slip off in the middle
of the afternoon, but...

Fuck you, mad workers!

Sleep and dreams and nothingness to you can't feed
the babies.
Drop the needle at 2:14 p.m. and there is Mingus Mingus
Mingus Mingus Mingus

Fuck you, mad workers!

Sleep and dreams and nothingness to ease the mind

2:14 AM AND THERE is MINGUS MINGUS MINGUS
MINGUS MINGUS!!!

DROWNING OUT YOUR SHIT!

Let the earthquakes come and erase all the work.

I'll step out back to trigger a Zippo and listen to the alley
music, too:

"Fuck you!

Fuck you!

You ain't gawn do shit!!"

Pop pop pop

Screech and grinding metallic humid breeze in trees

The sirens. The shots into the sky, the arm and at each
brick heat anger.
Squealing tires and then the worst:

The stomping feet of the neighbors and their inane
    conversations and
    trying not to scream.

Reaching for MORE…WHITE….NOISE….

Pynchon dashes upon the rocks, but Auster picking up
the brains with memories of NIGHTWOOD and WSB
in the wake, I wake…and one bird team won a nothing
game versus the last-place bird team.

Bike to the bar where the credit-card douchebags are
trying to learn about beer despite the twats of flavored
vodka and breathe in the errant streams of smoke from
the pipes of those that know better in the alleys of
knowledge.

Then it is home in different alleys, swaying in the night,
the moonlight, following the sirens toward that smell of
industrial fire and the glow of the far off sky.

Exhausted body loves on itself enough to drink faucet
    water.

Wednesday night. HOME.

Strip off the sweat soaked rags and drop the needle for
    the neighbors and

MINGUS MINGUS MINGUS MINGUS MINGUS.

DOWN LOW

Thinking he had something to prove,
he took on the night.
He took on the noise.
He took on the hill, the beer,
the whiskey, the challenges
of the youths. He shot.
He sipped. He chugged. He left.

He fought the hill.
The hill in collusion with gravity
met the swerve. The legs
of dipsomania failed.
But, it was only when he thought
of that delicious spot behind her ear
and the memory of her laugh.
Then he lost touch. Lost concentration.
It only took a second.
No longer atop the wheels,
he kissed the concrete.
Then he ran home with the handlebar
jabbing at his ribs.

Hemingway had three wives from St. Louis.
Gertrude Stein called him on it.

O.K. Best to keep the shotgun away
from the whiskey.
Sleep late or wake early
with the working idiots.

Cover the balls
before they suffer
another whack.

SECURITY BLANKET/WEB OF LIFE

How is life?
When all there is:
the foreseeable future,
all you drag behind
and what it equates to
in the eye, the place, inside there
in life
in heart
in perception to
be the soul
that is it.
That is you.
Take it.
Dress it up
in scheme and delusions.
Live with it.

I am father and banker.
I am latte-riddled corporate whore.
I'm the best lawyer money can buy.
I'm Christian, I'm starving and they don't care.
I'm a Luddite with a car and a computer.
I'm a joy to be around; these pills give me pleasure.
I just need my Fresca and my "Soaps".
I'm featherless sparrow in a ditch of treacle.
I'd rather be digging graves.
I only want to go to sleep.
I don't follow politics.
I just want to effect change.

I'm afraid of change and make beats with static, yo...

What else?
This can't be all, you know?

Slave pick cotton
make sneakers
harvest coffee bean.
CEO have peace-of-mind
make many families happy.

What else? Could be worse.

Many
more perspectives.

A realization:
that guy
that gang
that has never pondered.
Or have they?

Fear rises
that (t)he(y) might strike
that (t)he(y) might be able to take you
somewhere you don't want to go
and that's when you are no
longer free
with only a thought.
No know.
But that's not even
with you.

Subconscious tether
guides.
Lends actions to
ignorance ability
to fear
to kill
that something
other.

Bulk up police state.
"I love a man in a uniform."
Emasculate goat nature Zen,
manufacture Ken.
Interrupt interstitial space with cubicle
electric fence, defense system
24-hour lockdown
iron curtain
cold shoulder to comrade.

But seldom immediate
concrete
violent or physical.
"I don't need to fight
To proooove I'm right.
I don't need
to be forgiven!"

***

Sitting amidst spectators
capture moment that
nauseates

realization of pulsing
need of crowd for
more more more.
It
there on summer night
moonlight
breezes
music of insects
and
and
And
AND
yes,
there it is:
hunger and restlessness and confusion.
That: Mommy, I want some cotton candy.
That: Girl, gimme summa that ass!
That: Fuck, I need a fix.
That: I just want us to be happy, Sugar.
That: Ooh, Kill that motherfucker!
That: I hope he hits a homer, Daddy!
That: INNOCENT ALL-AMERICAN LUST.
Ask for it by name.

Try to relax amidst this
lust and longing
and be eaten or crawled
over, scratched apart and torn to shreds
for the sake of commerce, family, religion, politics
modern science
Better living through over-achievement!

But, come on! Paranoid freak!
There is no conspiracy!
Say "hello".
Relations will
communications will
HELL, maybe the liquor will
save the world.

Cross a line.
Walk into a backyard.
Introduce one folk
to another.
Try it, tie it
to one
another,
then tell me **Murdoch**
and Mickey
Mouse got some
power
and we're all drowning in toothpaste
when webs don't drown now
do they?

Get a pot luck goin'
with a bad dish
and LoQeusha
sayin' she got a brotha
in the can
and hands out the pop
'cause she don't drink.

Now how?

How now?

In that same neighborhood where
a sticker says, "Save the White Race"
and the poetry is co-opted,
church beds down with the state
but under the breath
know better.
It's only that some
are more adept
and comfortable with working
and taking orders and
some would rather rot
than take orders
kill than listen
blame than mourn
be guided than think
of other than
growth
mantra
growth
mantra
growth
mantra.

Kind, gentle
genocide over
communication.
Rub out poverty
in
"wealth."
People lost amidst

War as spectacle,
network ratings vehicle.
Extinction, trickle-down-effect
amidst
crowded and angry erections
of ordinary and conventional
make heap big cancer.

Him dead Indian
laugh, laugh, laugh.

Like some
gravy
on your
scapegoat, Dear?

Fine.
But, why must you be so negative?

Is that an ear in the pho-Buffalo gelatin?

Yes, like how cleanly it was removed?
Not oily in the least.
And you don't have to trim those
pesky hairs with rock
like Tonto did on sitcom!

You're the best cook, Tits!
You've really got the knack
for pho-food preparation.

No, Sugar Daddy, I read it in

Okrah Magazine!

Oh, ha ha ha ha.

But wait!
Empower
Slip past ignorance
to empathy.
Unclench the glass tit of fear
and see.
the bud on the tree
or the insect in the sand
that nihilist in the band
the man on the corner
that self-loathing loaner
that cunt on the third page
that prick with the road rage
is you.

That's what we are up to!

Sliver away cathode ray.
Chew off arm at shoulder,
leaving drunken whore of society
awash in torpid nightmare.

All in all. Minus one.
You view.
Drip dry from soma sauna from cathode ray
New view.
New you.
Now how?

WHAT?

Sit
Don't go down.
Smile
Don't know
Frown.
Wrap those lips
around my
Finger now,
Clown.

Ditch
that
Sun Down.
Don't
cry, Honey now.
Release the grip
around my finger.
There's a full moon
spilled with peach.
There's a shutdown
that I won't reach.

Moonlight shares
a common ground
with shade your being's
in.
Tear that shine
away to
see a dark side.

Tear that burning pole
and get a wet slide
lunge and stride
at the end
where reward
lies.

PAPERCUTCLIT

Plenty of Fish contemplating their existential
despair slobbed for a time
in utter laziness.

Getting really into cycling
skipped lunch, wolf down
both the red and the blue pills
failing to disclose certain taxable
income before the chigger bites
ruled the night.
They knew no better.

Would that he had clipped
his fingernailspapercutclit not in the mix:::
quiet secluded life.
Ugh.

DOSED JACKIE GLEASON EXPERIENCES

Your favorite:
"SPOT DREAM GLOT
WIENER GOT STINKER
LAY LOW DAY GLOW
ROBOT THINKER
PRINCESS PINK DRESS
ALAMO JEWELRY
12-STEP RAILROAD
FRENCH FRY CREEP"
is playing repeatedly on the jukebox.

A twelve-year old with a machete
and a hard on just gave his number
to the dishwasher.

Do you know what I mean?

Oh, yeah?
Seek help.
Remember this.
Learn to recite this.

If you can imagine
Groucho Marx being
God during helicopter flights
over reindeer herders
piss on fascists
with laughter
and THEN!!!

The dream continues!!

He went to the donkey farm
to get some ass
and found out all
silly twats were made
of putty.

Jackie was on a stool
next door.
He drank and gave Groucho
what for
What for?

ELF SHOT LAME WITCH

Scratching dog noggins through which the grey seeps
over the bugged-out eye of a dead squirrel
jittery from java response
to an incredibly efficient lunch
biked to and from
comes with the fall
and the final almond
under the desk chair
eaten for breakfast
ashes blinding the vision of your third eye
bored of health but tired of
sickness that might
devour gay style amidst
warrior tumbleweeds
ninja run down the airport stairs
singing about the end of paradise
until Anthony is needed in customer service
interrupted by an unsure deli worker
all started by a comfortable rising
and a leisurely workout while
the fraidy cats bark about televised
terrorism and seem proud, or unconcerned,
about martial law.

FINGERS NAIL

I need a pair of those gloves with ear holes where
icicles glow like the shine off patent leather Shoshones
from the people who brought you foam, gel, cement
paste in book form—you know, the handheld device.
She won't approve what with the vast progressions
given over the robins' weather and I look
up from my soup.
"DON'T PLAY WITH THE CRAYONS!
YOU'LL PUT THE FIRE OUT!" she screams.
I'm tempted to use a fork
to see what she's texting with those pretty,
polished weapons of vitriol
but I'm chasing the barley
to ward off starvation and make
little waves in the broth.

EATING MAMA LUCIA

Joking when he says they're playing
restaurant while the bald spot beer gut
is getting proprietary about a cocktail
table or a waitress or a wine glass
or a patch of land.

Grab that salt shaker
height brohouse full of churchmouse girls
squeaking like like like I feel like like like so,
anyway was a good movie but you forgot
about Antonioni and that actress who said
"So any way" should be one word?
"Soanyway," she said, with sand
on her tits and the house waiting to explode
in her mind.
Daddy issues much?

Water with your lemon like you do at home?
(deadpan delivery and a little smirk to slide
it past the dimwit).
Thoughts and daydreams
and applesauce all over the crying baby
would that it was Napalm.

Gonna drink that bottle
and watch Dexter later
after he escapes
with his pittance.

Last call shot time vaccine
for mental health
take the side streets into the back of the mind
curled up in the lizard brain
half aroused
in the sweetness of her lounging peach.

Or was that a dream and not an excuse
to eat frozen pizza at 6:15 in the morning.

CHAOS IS TASTY

If I could prove what cauldron or in which pot them smoke
over and damn shame angel hairs jostling on the blow hard
lips of Gabriel's pasta horn tooting a free lexicon two-tone
Ezekiel wheel when a balderdash Barthelme unit calling for
more ask Alice's Malachi record what he mean, him say—
"konk sense of 'mold' on the 'muff' sense of 'talk' on the
'surface' konk"—way back way way back on his piano stool
around and around on his piano stool before the pack hit
the new muse sick sticks reality fix for gasping fishnics in a
Gilligan gaff when he thought he might fornicate without
you or hurting Buck and DiMaggio sans Tai chi one on with
a girl-drink fetish given to part the thighs and start the lies
in a Tiki bar gavel the suffering travel the suffering innocent
lopped off like terrified ears what got an impetuous loop
down its gullet, an idea! fizzy on yer bum thank you very
much better thank you and a dollar more will get you
the mouthwash for gasping fishnics and gasping fishnics
sick sticks on the TV for a reality fix Barthelme unit of
like terrified ears what got impetuous loops and a handy
wipe oozed out from underneath your fisterrnails even
if they're nine inches See! I toldjuh what's the economic
sense of peace mission gone fishin' in the formaldehyde
gore his brain again and couldn't resist, stole a jigger and
swished it around his dentures to keep the night motions
juicy and smoothie and groovy loose the noose and fire
the victims and isms and fast for peace, 'cause you care
a dime to confuse last sensed or HOLD THE PHONE,
SWEET TITS just heard ghost dog those in a rut get 'em
on their backs and goosey goosey ash in the gash when
legs get legs get when legs all get akimbo coulda been a
wrapper in the breeze for a second and a granite taken for
surety by the nickelback robot in line for another whoopin'
and a skronk skronk on the deal it to Dinah Shore your
boatbutted harkens back to the bay where them waited out
the storm on hoppy suds and fresh fish, sand in the cracks
sure, but the safety to grit truly measured from head to
sweet, little stank by the seamstress in dream of algebraic
horndogs stuck like a lollipop with lotsa mustard while

Boots' stubble drips down on his axe diluted by sweat slobber off Scotchlip and water the drip drip bee drop a sloppy like a riff out of Akron honey inevitable sure with the clouds threatening could feel it seed and batten down the hatches, candles matches toasted just as reruns flicker out and you wish you woulda written home wish you would called and apologized to the Paiutes but fornicating to beat the ennui ploughing into and out of those daily rutso nutso bing bang times pigtails in the inkwell and then sloppy up against the coathooks postcards had to wait and now it is bang times pigtails in the inkwells ploughing into and outta Konk sense of mold on the muff way back way back against the coat hooks if she's lucky and that bald knobbin' don't allow no letters home too late now text from limbo and the faint sounds of a Griot riff if I could prove it would you listen to the jingle in the alligator purse?

POST BLUNT WITH THAT CRAZY GUITAR

Thoughts that interrupt dreams
you know what I'd like to do with this kid?
I'd like to throw a baseball to him
and see how many times I could be impressed
that he knew how to catch one.

I'm guessing that there would be some bruising involved
maybe a broken nose.

Worms thinking about dirt
Fish and water
Birds and breezes.

Yep. Still stoppin' to morph
into a pumpkin cake bar
at a truck stop
post blunt with that crazy guitar.

May be time for a nap in another thousand
Miles
Days
Nightmares.

LOVE IS HUH?

Mr. Assassin guy, lie concealed in the silence.
or
Flap your wings, Mr. Assassin guy.
Notice a glitchy screen
droll and subversive story
off by one flagged you for causing a ruckus?
Being one of the many askers of Huh?
I can attest.
But, you think you got it all there in your sights.

Well, let me tell you something, Mister.

You guys tend towards expensive sound systems
with a mannequin arm sticking out larger than
the rims of a massive 18-wheeler truck,
with a low loader stacked with cabinet speakers
twenty-feet high, connected to a turntable,
and you just pull a Sunn O))) album out
catch a glint of the full moon
drop the needle on the vinyl and faces
melt as the full force of a single drone chord
rips a hole in the space-time continuum
into the swirling void.

Lie concealed in the silence.
Gonna use love fingered into this velvet
Paisley sewing human teeth into monster dreams?
Feel like death, for you
see a mannequin arm sticking out
the recycling of a melodrama.

Scrambling on their hands and knees
to grab fistfuls of dollar bills thru expensive
pollution equipment trims about 15 minutes
off a typical journey with kids two years ago
only as part of a quaint, warm morning,
grooming routine.

Flap your wings, Mr. Assassin guy
by submitting a tip quickly and anonymously!
Kiss this economy on the horny face.
Soon, we ask: Huh?
There's nothing else but Huh?
There's nothing else but Huh?
There is no bigger promise than going out in a puff
    of Huh?
Love is Huh? Mr. Assassin guy.
You're not so sure of yourself now are you?

GRIEF HAS A SCENT AND YOGA

Pants are Destroying the Planet,
unless Jesus has an art show
with the runs close to your heart,
that German Peacock vase,
ramming the bullshit,
but at least it will be a shorter car drive.

Caught locally in a mob witch hunt,
there are lots of Mondays
and these goofy busboys
look a lot alike with a cool grown-up bib.
If they all had Megan's guts,
visceral in a way to fight forward
to this "wanted to do."

It (what is "it") can be just as nasty
like when bros are just mean and hostile,
but can give a damn good
"follow your dreams" speech
on fake gusto while beating back
despair and just remain,
unlike a rare photo of jazzmen,
confused with night screams,
the new fun of the kids.

While you were at it,
Isis sucked four toes
in a judgment Free Zone
organizing the footnotes rich

in the ace of your holes:
that extravagant hope of youth
and a concerned girl,
(both the coolest and scariest)
pushed the stools in at an odd angle
against a fully murdered out beat up sedan.

NOW! The crabby ladies at the Drive-In
are gunning for her!
I feel like Hillary Clinton is LITERALLY
shitting her pants!!!

Tesla's magic children helping
Charity Cornhole Tournament clowns
not under investigation,
elation and humbled-devastation
with bi-curious unicorns
or on any swing set
or in a microwave at play
on our life spancake terrorist
poles are not on our watch list
for waffle toppings.

Grief has a scent and Yoga pants
are destroying the planet.
This according to a dollop of fear
mongering algorithm goin' clackity
clack next door, ya know?
So can houseplants at a venture
capital firm with some silly older fellow
and sure enough, the living crow
mounted the dead one.

POOTIE TANG AND JOHN CAGE

Outside of the morgue-think and a huge dump trailer,
in the forbidden depths of a massive thought,
it would be best to ease privileged scolds
from downed power for long-term play
in a Halloween costume and a 1949 sedan
where people love a dry ass:
only mildly incapacitating a plumber
for a rather easy job on a long-haul
with a birdy reading INFINITE JEST
on a newfangled flip phone.
Thirty miles in, there was a conversation about
    solar shithouses.
Nine months later: you know the rest.

When the twin girls' mother called the school's
sassiest yucca plants salad
IT was very rare to see whatever it takes
including special requests, in a timely
and consistent manner:
Evil for second hand is a rallying cry
for pragmatists long thought of by society
as conspiracy theorists and kooks everywhere
after FEET WORN FROM WORK.

Scrubbed those clean young
and with the mothers of families
where nothing happens and everything happens
and a bit of radio blooming is hard,
and the most important thing is that electrotherapy

was used to treat soldiers and the pre-pubescent
as the world sounded 100% like a child.
Fart magic. Belch beautiful.
You gotta grab society by the ears.
You gotta look it in the eyes.
You gotta clean out its ears
and give it the lay of the land.
Tell us the similarities between Pootie Tang and John Cage.

JOE FREEMAN IS COMING HOME!

I WISH HE COULD FLY

Bob's down for affliction.
Maybe have a wank
with a wallaby
or not.
It's a thought.
Able to help with mental
yoga and flossing
and the affectations
of lots and lots.

We have rats, unfortunately.

Man, I wish he could fly.

Why let cost be a concern?

Real good at being a gofer
and smashing
your televisionminds
and granny's twat
is made of silly putty.
She knows it's funny.
Is there an echo in here?

Man, I wish he could fly.

After a nap in the sand
it becomes apparent
they're not so happy.

They can hardly count
that they're leaving the band
to move on to a new relation
with something like Syd
in the outback.
But, not gonna ride the gravy train
and know that someday
they're gonna say that they miss
the buffet at the anarchist cafe
and the urgency in the photographer's
eye on the morning
after a radio show broke
the little toes of a mind.

Man, I wish he could fly.

Bill punched fries today and the biceps
are happywhappy, Pappy.
Almost suspicious
to better check under the sea
turning into a cartoon
version of themselves.

Why let cost be a concern?

Thinking before speaking
more like saying
"I don't know."

She escaped outside so she
could smell where she's supposed
to be, thanks to the college

wrestling fans and lack of impetus
from humanity on a slab minus
the phone holder.

Befriending a fascist
only to put it in a blender
and make magic means
Belch&Felchslap reality, Folks!
Abort memory.

Why let cost be a concern?

Mommy Might Prefer Jazz.
It is time to make a new world.

Do as I said, not as I did.
Is there an echo in here?

A sturdy little steamer
right now would save this show,
Dude.

When older, he did it silently,
said sharks Might Prefer Jazz
to Other Types of Music
or others well-suited for any adventure
in the night side-by-side who raids
with some rookie in spring training
for the growth of the bacteria
who can't lay down a bunt
or fathom the hit-and-run
that causes botulism

immediately publicizes minivans
aren't usually considered hipwack
whack but deemed
the highest in hierarchy rude
slang literally to defecate
while still wearing one's clothing.

Why let cost be a concern?

Sally hopes the bosses need you
to pull over the DEATHSTAR
right now or else she's going
to sell pants with us
for the first time in a pyramid
scheme on such a night.

Man, I wish he could fly.

That's something of a stone
if for one fast one
and on a slippery slope
of who knows what's right to drop off
so your rascal
doesn't take a shot.

Why let cost be a concern?

(What is that? Tofu?)
Keep it coming.
I dun toldya wunce!!!
and then she'd cup
your balls,
say, "Love yourself."

Well, so far, The Witcher is scoring fairly high
on the all-around "bonkers" scale
and it is only the third inning
and maybe this is a dream
during a Bob Uecker and Jack Buck
rain delay session
or a glitchy cloud seance conjuring
Dean Martin
and Buddy Hackett.

MISSING THE MANATEES

Now that my teeth are falling out
and I feel close enough to angelic visions,
I can share a gruesome modern thriller
that incorporates science with a rust-resistant
vision of a 14-year-old animator
AND all the big corporate leviathans
missing the manatees and the foundation
of Republican fundraising suggested due
to limited capacity is now in comic form.

You can kill terrorists, with education.
A gooey load with a lot of personal sadness
looks at the world of espionage.
Film at 11.

WHAT'S NEXT?

Flexibility is more important than buffets
and the book scientists suggest a dog's
asking for sex,
accepted the part on the condition
that boy's drawing of a golden peacock
despite the woman saying no to him,
he continued to ask her questions
and pet her cat.

Everclear, some foliage charges say
that's not a question
wildly into the woods, passing the naked
William and the book
snacking on competing
and not just trying
Sit down ... and figure out what's next

MAYBE SOMEDAY, BUT NOT...

You glow and
I taste you
in the moonlight mud.
My tired lips remember
you in a way that
would disgust your husband
and confuse your children.
If your fruit hung on trees
populations would go mad
like they do
and populate deserts
never wanting for water,
salve or spices.

And I feel no shame
in these dreams.

But to make them best
we would have to align tiger stripes
on the shade of the moon.
Shuffle logic;
Break the flying buttresses of
ancient architecture;
Finger fuck Shakespeare fans
on CNN.

All fun and reckless activities: all dangerous.

We would be better to
change society and
inject vodka into nuns
or swill melted nickels with
actuarial cubicle door knobs.

So I know that you do.
I know that I do.
We do.
As the swelling goes down,
we don't.

I hope that there is something.
I hope that there is a part.

There it is in the glimmer of a star.
I hear it in the sublime verse.
I hear your moans as my back creaks.
I hear the echoes of promises.

THOUSANDS OF YOU

My heart my soul
Dig a ditch and shit each day
Weigh a livelihood and sanity
With logic and the need for something other
Maybe a love and a life and we can be next to
The great American dream.

Get a drink
You do
Was it a Grey Goose?
But I've got a need
and you've got a need
and we've got a need.
Maybe in the next world.

But not in this one
and I thank you for
not bothering to
waste my time.

ODE TO THE FANATIC

There is no funny racism
or runny fascism
while ye prisoners of hope and fall colors
eat pumpkin-spiced cold meds and mucous to
avoid neti pot death
hot dogs and waitresses
flying in every direction.

Put wastoids in your booster
Load ether with lead-addled muckmuck.
Cough up gravy into your designer tissue.
Club gravitas.

Oh, and Ichabod's head is off the top
of the visitor's dugout and kangarooing
up the aisle in that horse's ass.
Van hit the soybean head
shoot dead boy stranger danger
inexperienced eagle gorged on afterbirth

Root for the one percent in your muumuu.
Chug aluminum –bottled water and hoot.
Live it up. Toss lewd verses to garbage.
Your days are few. Your wool is worthless.
Replay these days and they'll go back and look at it
stored on yourtube or reflected in a mirror coffin
or another threat to the environment babbling
DADA in a six-wheeled stroller.

Would that we could all slip
            on our corporate muumuus
and waddle into the stadium
                    with such unity.
Oh!!!
  to capture the inner thigh sweat that melds
        with nacho cheese
            scraped off with a $175 ticket stub
      purchased
with corporate funds.

FAIR WARNING

After the pain and suffering
in result of your own actions
occurs more often
you will begin to talk to yourself
as if you were your Mom
or girlfriend.

"Careful now, Honey!
You remember what happened
last time!"

IN TWISTED SHEETS

The thunder sounded the third nightmare
caused me to rise and shower off
my eyebrows easily.
The kink in the neck caused the second dream in
white noise of fan breeze and AM radio
static and banter.
A vision of candles dripping onto your birthday
crab cakes under your delicious pout and
a violet sky, swirling counter-clockwise
highlighted the first dream before we knew of
the unrest to come in twisted sheets.

SAFE

If I felt like favoring verbose
to donning the habits of
Sister Mary three-eyed albino
frog in the Chesapeake Bay
of your yuppie condo toilet
finger fucking your asphalt-paved
cruelty in the memory of
Sitting Bull
failing Safe is where I keep my Cuban missile crisis
half-dollars
Where I slip Elvis' bones gasoline spewing
into Sterno-lined porcupine cunts
in the back seat of an asbestos-flavored
car bomb.
George Bush is either punk rock
or wreckslop pissing off more Muslims
than you can shave your dick with an
arrowhead sinking into quickmudsoaked
blood notanymore land or sea can you say
Who gives a fuck?
Shit and cram your cock in it 'cause you're in love with
yourself, autoerotic ashphalt dildo
Coming on your own daydream
down the throat of your favorite reality
Flavored with spearmint julep
Love slave twiddling uranium clits
of backstabbing soccer mommies
that shit on the chest of the suffragettes
by electing warmongers out of

neurotic Sunday night Lifetime Channel
Fear.
Four beers, six shots and a mad cow sandwich
in ten minutes for lunch.
I'll toothpick my own eyeballs and drop
them in your martini with some LSD
Ebola urine.
Tip me on that, you dim sum-slurping cretin!

LET'S SELL THIS TO THE UNTWIDDLED
CLITS OF BEJESUS

For those whose lawns drink
more than they do,
whose minds are smothered in
busy-ness, cathode and the
moss of self-help;
Whose souls are crushed
by dogmatic vines,
bullshit never
takes a holiday
nor ceases shooting its
wad on the
face
of truth.
In every other liar's film
made with a filthy, fucking lens
held by a
masturbating twit-git bored, dim-sum slurping
ass
a blitzkrieg called patriotism
insures that
the dump pump hump
is still
injecting
collagen into flaccid, lifeless,
lustless,
ignorant, jitter-fucking latte slaves
that go strutting
insect-free to the rapid-fire drum beat of
landfills under condos and $20,000 Volkswagens.

A piss-soaked woman gone mad screams
in a cathedral of
tourists
the only commandment,
"Don't be an asshole!!!!"
as shutters click
and the intelligence of man
pays for a better set of tires
and some water-resistant rain gear
plus a meteorologist's salary and
some wheat grass pills run through
bowels of an Asian pussy cat with
a bumper sticker.
I skim the want ads, singing hallelujah
that the perfect job doesn't want me
asphyxiating in a two-car garage
or
buying a scope for a rifle and shoes
good enough to climb that tower
as the roasted Thanksgiving turkey necks
gobble gobble up department store
cunts.
That'll be $49.95. Thank you. Please cum again.
And the urinary tracts of the
barking security alarms
are in perfect health
as she writes out a
check for more safety.

So cackle and
jack-off through the crackup.
Masticate over an armpit soup

while dickheads of wigs swilling
their own cumaidsicle juice drip drop
aids virus tick tock
and the sick cops
slip chafed cocks in foreign crabgrass
articulated pussvortex
whores draped in velvet
because.

I LIKE THIS LESSON

You could drive yourself DAILY
crazy if you think too hard
about what life owes you
the various entities that owns
you.

Ozone and you people
and so in your life
owe you daily crazy.

Try not to worry too much daily
crazy and so about it.

In fact, forgiveness
is the best possible
course of action
now too hard about daily
weekly crazy
if you think.

Minutely

Balance out a joint chapbook
who control finance
vaguely wander forward,
in that American boastfulness
is like that of small boys
in television nature shows
and an ardent spokesman

for conservation and protection
of endangered animals
like someone waking up
live every Tuesday night
to a crowd packed with dancers
and vaguely wondering
and so and so
in the dark.

The stew is becoming
itself as I sip
this afternoon's advice.
Kill a device.
Don't learn how to use it.

This is the modern wayday.

A CHURCH PEW, AN ALMA MATER,
AN EMPLOYER,
A CREATIVE COLLABORATION,
A BED OR A BEER.

Communication is key today.
Blabber Things
as if you are the best.

Food looks good.
Maybe that's where I get it from:
in my mirror.

We had pork chops.
 Who ordered me a moon lamp????

Worried it might be a surveillance device.

Not a joke
stopped by to buy parts
for his gun and ended
up also buying ammo
in a helicopter
and dropped Buffalo
Wild Wings gift cards
on the rioters?

Are we going well?
Bitching at the television?

Stop.

Remember.
There can be meals.
There can be thoughts.

But, you're sure to improve
them even more with a few
well-placed words,
Ragers.

A quick e-mail or impromptu meeting
can make a big difference!
Communication is key Communication
watching cops take selfies with the terrorists.
Improv is the key
to get
down the bunny hole.

Things are sure to improve
to the mind of the idiots
and so even more with a few well-placed
succulents in the garden of Karen.

Expecting it up to the trumpertrumpeters
there is going to be some phlegm
going dark for a while
in the Wednesday capital show
gang with guns part a big improvement
improv key communicationation
nation improve
if blibber blabber.

Was it a surprise?

Sure even if you do, so
in the images of insurrection flashing
across the screen, then what?

Nothing happened.
It was all about ratings.
Err, I mean raisons?

Remember that Super Bowl commercial?

PFASCISM DEATH AND DANDELIONS

Stayed with her for a couple of days...
towards the end of her days.
She was on whoknowswhatdrugs
they give to old people
who ate too much pie
in houses backed up
to cornfields.
We were zoned out
on some TV show one afternoon.
She turned her head
and looked out
through the front window;
like, a picture window.
"Those people are never
gonna leave or find what
they're looking for if
they don't accept their lies."

I turned my head,
stood and turned.
There was the yard
of many childhood days,
childhood, find good memories.
Now, mostly weeds spiced
with Dandelions.
Better, but reminding me of stupid,
slave labor and the core of fascism:
Family.

"I never did ride a bicycle," she sighed.

I looked back at her.
She smiled.
Had the clicker in her hand.

Shot me
with the urge to watch
more television.

PERHAPS (because, Gertrude Stein)

Perhaps, perhaps, I was not meant to be formed
Formed perhaps was I not meant to formed be
    performed
Perhaps dreams my distress me at being
Being something is
Only My perhaps I
Eye inside eye
Return something nothing more
I inside me nothing more
Me inside I more nothing have
Perhaps, perhaps I bore, I swore
Inside me nothing more
How is life to the core?

Life is
How life is
Is life
and life is how is how is is
The foreseeable how is
All drag behind you
and All you behind drag how and is how I how I now
    I now

I know I be
I formed
and what it equates to me makes nothing how is nothing
in the eye is how and how is life is perhaps, perhaps,
I was not meant
Only
My

More return nothing
and there and I am why
and for sure nothing and inside nothing more
and in the eye, the place, the more nothing
in life
In perhaps and nothing on the maybe and the taste
    that on a cracker
and not that's a real frosting
Love it to me.

In all as is it as is as is yet make it all as can be
That its it be one.
Why you be soul?

I've got all the power
I've got all the power
I'm oozing of the EVERYTHING!!!!!!

Take all
Dress it up
In scheme and delusion
Up take and when then all scheme all and when all
    delusion
Poop diaper

And I told this and I do not know.
And as exactitude then as proportions as trains as
    trains as trains
As father and lost child strains
And fuck and nothing lost as he sees it.

And as still I must as live with with it.

ROTATE YOUR TIRES

Negative Nellies and Sweet Polly Purebreds,
He-Men, bullhorns, underdogs, clicking mice and fraidy
cats, Cronkites, security cams and helmets, safety
    goggles
and empathy
true love and gravel fucks
don't stop the wars hawks drop and
the rain of bloody injustice in the dustbeltistan
as you flip through the channels and pages
looking for the rest
of the wrestling of your mind
in the high definition specs that
fail to capture the cosmic slop.

A wedding ring and the keys to the minivan
when daddy's taken for a goose ride
and we're all conked out like Mr. Van Winkle
makes no nevermind to the vortex or the fish tails
    because
The Viet Cong didn't watch the Waltons
and Good Times so you could buy
cheap tee shirts and the scrap metal Coca-Cola cans
from a ground zero china shop away from the bull
of Wall Street.

So flit around in the mind of Billy Pilgrim
or pretend we fed turkeys to helpless savages
and that the radios help us
consider all things in mid-commute from
cubicle to air-conditioned podcast twitter feed
facsimile of life.

Change your tires
Change your oil
Change of scenery
Change your mind
Change for a dollar
Loose change?
Sex change?

Feel better?
Well, if you weren't full of shit,
you'd be changing your pants.

So there's something.

If you think too much about the difference
between the damage you have done and the
frugality that you promise yourself,
remember that shrink-wrapped vegetables
and leaf-blowers ARE FUCKING RIDICULOUS!
...and so are you.

Ha!

Manageable decisions and necessary delusions
at all other times.
Or...
Is it reality for you?

History confirms our banality
stupidity
and destructive proclivities.
...and all the time pimpin', is in effect.

You know what I'm sayin'?
Bitch better have my money!

Take a dose of satire when needed.
Baffle the dumb-ass.
Kiss a smart-ass of your liking.

...and prepare to be chastised.

Take care of yourself.
The only real control we ever
have
and need
is with self...

and the self is a fallacy.

...BUT! when you can manage,
remember
the only commandment,
according to the bag lady in the cathedral:
DON'T BE AN ASSHOLE!

Oops!
Too late?
Well, here's this:
Focusing on what you don't want
brings it to you.
So watch out!
You're gonna die.

SPRINGTIME!

It's mid-morning as
the fat lady plops down the steps
huffing and puffing towards the car
gasping for air
arms all akimbo.
Hootin', "Woooo, have mercy. Lawd, Dear God!"
Fannin' herself with the three fingers free
from her oversize bag.
Scuff shoes shufflin' across the pavement now
until one falls off.
Perched on one leg; draped in a muumuu;
she stops to slip it back on
the front of her swollen foot
that won't squeeze in over the heel.
No Cinderella dreams today.
"Move it, Bitch!" screams the driver.
"We a'ready late!"

But she doesn't lose her balance
as bird chirps and the smell of mowed grass
and gasoline
float in on a cool breeze.

The bartender rolls over
and turns up the radio.
Somebody is angry that the relief
staff won't be enough
for the Fall
classic.

He gives it up.
Gets up.
Shuts the window
and realizes
that he stripped naked
before crashing in front
of the fan
last night.
Howdy, Neighbor!
He chuckles.
But no one is around.

FORGET WHAT ARGUE MEANT

Bootstompin' lawnmowers
and asphalt slaves
Young and dumb
and it gets things done
Rile up the masses!
Chocolate milk could be banned
Understand the motivation of a common theme
But you can't argue
with the pistils and the petals

VANITY

Big day and an early wake-up
on a frigid January morning
to make the best of what's left,
the poet grabs the towel
and catches himself
through the post-shower fog
in the long mirror on the bathroom
door.

Still groggy, he thinks
that he still looks good enough
for a barely employed, aged
and single guy
who lives a bit rough and tumble
and needs a space heater
to keep his feet warm
some nights.
At the right angle if you squint
0 0 0
Whatever.

He towels off and applies
various ointments to problem
spots or areas.
Wipes down the walls
and hangs the towel on the rod.
Gets himself panted, socked and shod
in front of the news on the monitor
and returns to what's left of the warm
steamy room to shave.

There he is!
The mirror over the sink under three
bright lights does not forgive.
He starts off with more hot water
lathers up and begins thinking
now of the eyes of his family
and the wrinkles of time around them
and the flecks of skin too tough to be
removed by water
under the unkempt, grey hair.

When he clacks the Gillette off
the porcelain again, the cartridge
pops off and goes straight down
the drain.
Ha!

Time for a change, anyway,
though it takes time for him
to locate a new one.
Disorganized
in his chilly space.
Squinting into various closets
and then remembering the drawer
where he put his kit.
In the kitchen?

He's having cataract surgery today.
The right eye will be as good
as the left later in the day.
At least that's the plan.

His joke is: if they botch
the surgery, he'll be a one-eyed
drunk poet with a bit of a chance
to find a simple job.
Because, if you squint and turn
the mind in a certain direction,
little can beat him, but
it sure would be a nice time
for some green tea
and a shot of whiskey
with some boiled eggs.

No No
not before surgery.

SIRENS

*The problem with these people is
their cities have never been bombed and
their mothers have never been told to shut up.*

-Charles Bukowski "TROUBLE"

They hardly come as a surprise anymore
Those storm and air raid warning sirens
that sound at 11 a.m. on the first Monday
of every month.

Oh, there's a second or two when
they cause alertness
to be sure.
But, I miss the effect
the "alarm" they have caused
in the past.

Tend bar all weekend.
Close out Sunday by attending
the reggae spin at the local bistro.
A regular happening not so much
for the music, but for the crowd
the relaxing vibe.
In short, the perfect environ to wipe
the slate clean and swallow
necessary delusions
that ALL IS WELL
shedding some of the blood money
and sinking back into the neighborhood
and its gossip.
A destination, they call it.

Attention set on it while closing
and cleaning the bar, downing
jiggers of whiskey
several cigarettes
more pints of ale in anticipation
knowing I had Monday
to recoup.

Then I would jump into someone's
car or cab or bus
or ride the bicycle to finish
the night off.

The dub still happens
and somebody is still smoking
bowls in the back basement hall.
But, it is not me.
Not quite as often.

Miss those summer mornings
Awakened by sirens
through open windows.
Startled and sweating
and wondering immediately
if they had finally come to save us
from our consumer nightmare
or if a colossal funnel cloud
approached to blow it all away.
But, more importantly,
WHERE ARE THE PANTS?
THE KEYS?
THE SHOES?

THE BICYCLE?
And how the hell did I end up
HERE?

Now, after returning
from the gym to kick up the thermostat
Shower
Shave
The sirens do their duty
but the heater and the closed windows
muffle the surprise
and the car keys are right where I left them.

DAY

In silence after vultures bickered over
the dead armadillo,
He rose and yearned, slurped and
put on the sky inside out
squinched his nose
donned his shoes stuffed his
mitts in his hip pockets
snot nosed and weary sensing
a bunch of sumac and sassafras
listening for a distant cry of
a wasp or whippoorwill
a crane, a bird of any other
kind
even a train whistle,
or the light of a star.

When finally came the faint whisper,
with a twist of his fingers on the
knob
a voice on the radio
across the sleeping souls
and educated pisswillies of doom
boiled in the urine of virgin boys.

Vicious gobs of phlegm
a damn leak in the engine roof
up a spider's ass halved
open with a torch
and after awhile

it went to sand
and they beat the dried leaves
of the lady's slipper into a powder.

Cackled and slapped his thigh
but missed the fly
used a mixture of chimney soot
and lard.

The old timer shut his trap,
accentuated with a solemn nod
and a puff of the stub of a
cigar

"It ain't your Friday yet, Boy."

HOW FAR DOES THE HEAD SWIVEL

The hawk's shadow is motionless
high in the limbs
against a winter haze
above the alley as he peers
off the back porch
inhaling the ghosts of friends
some of them dead
through the filter

11 p.m.

He is waiting for it to pounce
and wonders if it is instead an owl
as the neighbor
to the East lets his
hounds out
and then back in
when the beast with wheels
to support crippled hind-quarters
yelps

Silence returns
as he gazes at faint Christmas Eve stars
and sips the last of the Imperial Stout
a gift
wondering how the urban bird's vision
differs from his

Bones aching from the clench of
the steering wheel

along winding roads
mind easing from the
white
line
fever
caught from the country hills reunion
and the stress of the holiday week

He is only sure that he is
where he is

Innards wrestle with the dichotomy
of lost childhood idiocy
and a huge meal
while his head swims in thoughts
of a dead father and the quote
his mother included on the
card
from Hafiz
something about God's yearning for
"the playfulness in your eyes"

The sluggish impulse to denounce
tradition
and hopes that he is choosing
the correct path
in delicious cocktails
complete the dilemma

South St. Louis dreams
as the head swivels and
the eyes shine

BASE DREAM

Heat-riddled in centerfield
thinking of the future,
thinking of her,
thinking of nothing but
the steel springs of action
and poetry-in-motion;
that motherfucking umpire and
last night with Dee Dee in Tulsa.
She, putting it on me after 12 innings;
Pulling the gauze off my strawberries
with her teeth.
When a slashing roundhouse
catches the business end of
an Adirondack
arching down in a quick and smooth
motion and CRACK!
I can tell by the sound of it
that it is coming my way
and I am galloping with
my back to it—
halfway to the point
where I know it is going
to land if I don't make it
when I step in a hole
fit to bury a cat,
then spring up
like a bony slinky,
take three adrenaline-fueled,
impossible strides
and lunge twice my length.

At the end is my reward:
A horsehide snow cone
in my Trapeze webbing.

SPORTING PAIN

I used to have a fastball. Clocked at 87 miles-per-hour once or twice. It was no ticket to fame, but not bad for a lanky teenager. It used to dive under the mitts of catchers and rise enough to cause Major League scouts to cause notice when they spied my High School stats. I threw crooked and left-handed and struck out a lot of country boys in the sunlight and under bad lighting on dirt fields. Meanwhile, I learned to drink rank lager out of cans along gravel roads and sometimes on the next day, I'd pitch again, sore arm or not.

I threw a no-hitter the day after prom night my junior year. I remember the second baseman pounding OJ and groaning in the seat across from me in the bus that Saturday morning, bitching about his weariness, his hangover, the sun and the noisy-ass bus. I could be wrong, but I think he went three-for-four that day and we won in five innings. He wasn't bitching and moaning on the ride home. I remember that for sure. We rode home giddy and cocky and goofy as fuck.

When I was in Little League, we only played a dozen or so games a summer. I had nothing to do but keep score during the KMOX broadcasts of Cardinals games when they were agonizingly close to first-place, but never there in the end. I'd spazz out in my bedroom amidst posters of Kenny Reitz, Ted Simmons, Bob Gibson and other out-of-town legends such as Johnny Bench and Willie Mays, bouncing balls off the walls and diving around to test my agility and ability while Lou Brock stole base after base, free agency took effect in the Major Leagues and I busied myself in between pitches. Occasionally, the games would show on television and I'd watch with my Dad, who turned me onto the history of the game by showing me around a board and dice game called Strat-O-Matic. I could manage the '74 Cardinals and test my luck against the '54 Giants or the '27 Yankees, managed by my father. We played catch and he threw me batting practice and took me to games at Busch Stadium. We would be there in time to enter as soon as the gates opened and stay for the last pitch, often waiting outside the clubhouse doors to gather autographs. Every loss was agonizing to me. I was only a frustrated fanatic.

I rode along on bus trips with the high school team when I was a little dude and Dad was the coach. I liked the sound of spikes on concrete and the rattling of the wood bats in the canvas bag…the pop of the mitt, the crack of the bat, the smell of Atomic Balm, the sign language between coaches and players and grass-stained baseballs. I liked the different consistencies of dirt and the relief of water when my mouth was dry and my face was covered in dust after a long ride on gravel roads with the windows down.

Baseball is a sensory experience. It stings, it burns, it aches, it itches and it sings with adrenalin in your veins when your motions fit with the poetry of the game. When you kick it, drop it, throw it away or in the dirt, swing and miss it or pop it up, it hits you in the gut worse than Montezuma's revenge. The agony of defeat is real. I prefer getting nutted by a bad hop to the feeling following a loss that I could've prevented. But I prefer both of those feelings to getting upset while watching from the sidelines. Especially when it is the fate of a bunch of millionaires hanging in the balance.

If you give a shit, the game will take all you got and throw it right back in your face, sometimes in the form of dirt, crow, humiliation and disgust. Other times, you get something back that was worth the blisters, wind sprints, shin splints and strawberries. My desire to master the game was enough to get me out of the cornfields and into a university. When it all ended at the end of my junior year in college, my pitching elbow fucked with tendonitis, I was a lost soul for years, but I still knew that life was worth a lot of physical pain when you get to the other side of achievement. Over twenty years later, I struggle to understand what life is like for those who don't bother to bust out of inertia. I love the comfort of a good rut. Don't get me wrong. Coasting, gliding, piggybacking, oh yeah—that's good stuff, too. I'll even admit to some corner-cutting and half-assing from time-to-time. I learned a lot about those methods while enduring certain days of practice when I wasn't feeling well, or was nursing a sprain or a strain. I also learned that if you play through a little bit of pain, your mind will adjust and you can get the job done. Then you'll be in a better place while your muscles burn and your back aches. The skunkiest, pisswater beer tastes all right in a place like that, but if you don't want one of those hangovers, drink the good stuff. Pain does not always lead to gain. Sometimes it leads to suicide and bad poetry.

Which leads me to an important point: getting rid of the pain of fun gone stale. The hangover is an unfortunate side effect of laziness. Yes, you have to drink and maybe smoke and avoid drinking healthy amounts of water to achieve the existential dread of the hangover, but laziness only prolongs its power. Do you enjoy being the whiny bitch or groaning loner after every night at the pool hall, wedding reception, wine-soaked book club meeting? I'll be honest, I do good work while hungover and enjoy long bouts of solitude, so I don't avoid hangovers. From my observations, though, most of you are different, so here is some advice: get some exercise. A brisk walk will re-oxygenate your body and pump out the poison. Drink lots of water. It will never taste better. A run or bike ride evict the demons. Soon you will feel like as if you are truly living. That is only the effect of some tricky chemicals in your brain. You will still be the same cog in the belly of the beast, but it will feel much better once you've rejuvenated yourself and are able to face reality. In other words, fuck the game, don't let the game fuck you! Get up and do something about it and be ready for next time. These sound like mad exhortations of a meth-addled wrestling coach, but their reasoning is sound and worth carrying out.

Of course, there is the realm of pleasure in the sack to relieve your aching brain. My favorite way to spend a day after a night of fun is to fill it with more fun. Get friendly with a leisurely hedonist who absolutely has to have two things in the morning: sex and food. Blow off class or work or and class and get to it as soon as you wake up. Nothing like it, Folks: the windows open and the sounds and breezes lowing in over your two-backed beast—its visit lasting until it is time to visit your favorite wok, bistro, pub, tavern or diner. A workout following chow! Good living, for sure, especially considering that a shower and more of the good stuff are excellent appetizers and desserts. Of course, that is the advantage of leisure and many of you bolt upright to the sound of his or her alarm clock, too late to enjoy such mornings, but you've got to do something to jettison the malaise and madness. Let them run off to work if they have to or get the hell away from them if they can't or won't perform in the morning (or afternoon).

Here is a vision of your future should you skirt the world of physical exertion: you may well stop drinking.

I know, that sounds crazy, though many around you are crazy enough to practice abstinence and are being coaxed into such behavior by lots of advertising and a kazillion-dollar-a-year drug industry, not to mention an all-encompassing police state. So barring something obscene and deadly such as going dry, you might become one of those folks who is enamored with computer games, statistics, and lo-cal desserts. You'll suffer gastric difficulties due to stress from watching sports for its results without any regard for the beauty of the game itself. Your anxiety will be heightened by your appetite for tri-caffeinated cans of death which you will sometimes cut with vodka so that you don't strangle the idiot you're dating. OR! Or, you could possibly become so devoured by the cult of fantasy leagues that well… let's not go there.

Yes, many favor delusions and illusions to rational thought and following a path of reason. Some speak of unicorns and Santa Claus. They drink the "blood of Christ" and go home to bleed internally over a sports event without any regard for the beauty of the game itself. A morning will come when you realize you are one of the numb nuts you used to hate: that frustrated fanatic who screams at the TV.

Believe me. It's true. C'mon, you can save those activities for when you're doped up on state-ordered soma in some geriatric hovel.

Don't say no! Enjoy the nightlife and physical activity while you can. The stress will kill you before a little sensory stimulation…and if you do find yourself in need of a good, drying out spell, you're going to need to sweat that out with some good, outdoor huffing and puffing, if not a little heave-ho!

If you can stand to get out of bed, that is.

COP DRANK PISS

She put kimchi on cheese sandwiches
and was proud of her nasty streaks
She had a sense of humor
despite it all and an appreciation
for the theatre of the absurd
like that scene
in DUMB AND DUMBER
where the cop drank piss.

Out at night
Up in the air
She drifted
into the mother fuckin'
stratosphere!

Amazing,
like midnight
in a daisy

Unlikely,
Dazed
less-than-once
Nightly.

She fell prey
to envy
She fell prey
to greed
Lying alone in darkness,
she fell prey to need.

FINGERS REMEMBER

Do you know the days
when you look at the orange
and it is not gonna happen?

Peeling a fucking orange
is too difficult
same thing with a boiled
egg.
You had the nightmares.
You made it to the bathroom.
THEN!
Your fingers remember.
Taste.
Hot sauce on the soft
boiled egg.
The explosion of juice
from the orange.

DEPRESSION is something.
Taking a walk around the park
is a cure.
Whiskey and Hemingway
Spelled wrong, though?
Whitchway do we go?

…and you wake up and hear
Pop Pop say, "so DRIVE HER TO THE HOSPITAL!
SHE'S GONNA NEED HER SHOE."
Checked out the track listing

and funny hearing him saying
all things that way.
Are you in the back stretch?
Keep kicking!

CHUCK BARRIS DIED FOR YOUR SINS

Gotta box lunch now
in the fascism rain.
The best movies
on the phone and
the theatre
closed.
History and hysteria
fuck in the dust
and we've got more stuff.

The ejaculate stream
on the airwaves spits
its poison
into the vacant minds of
of the blind, toothless
eagle cooks are driving
because there's more traffic.
History and hysteria fuck
in the dust in the memory
of Jay P. Morgan's
wicked grin.

The tweeters
wouldn't know a good film
if it bit them on the tip
of their underfed
jizztubes.
Dust in their memories
a hysterical muck.

Meanwhile, the jackhammer
rains suicide breakfast
for those who crave sunshine
and the lavatory attendants
scream into the raindrop
soup of sycophantic convulsions
about the fantasy conventions
of peeking into toilet stalls
the thought of memory:
history and hysteria
fuck in the dust.

The hooker pumps like
Alan Hale, the skipper
from Gilligan's Island.
Arms all akimbo
to put her corpulence in
motion that her legs
alone won't muster.
History and hysteria fuck
in the dust.

Down the street
to hustle for anything
but another trick
that requires walking funny
into another broken-glass morning's
cheap operations
for a cheap, foodless
meal for a fuck
in the dust.

Daylight is burning
and nights are wasted.
Tasted like cemetery mounds
for those left in the places
where there is still
something like there there
in the high school halls
where we dreamt of topless
barbers who refused dates
pulling the high note
down from the Arctic circle
with a spastic colon.

Not the patting on the back;
not consolation.
Leave the streets to their
commerce or erase the soul
while history and hysteria
fuck in the dust.

GET OUT GET OUT
See it with bourbon.
GET OUT GET OUT
Tell all your friends!
GET OUT GET OUT
See it again.
Wonder what GET OUT II
will tackle.

Can't move to Canada.
While history and hysteria
fuck in the dust,

but we can break those
tea cups and throw away
those spoons.

While history and hysteria
fuck in the dust
and if life's a bowl
of cherries
then what's death?
an avocado?

Snickering... "oh....no.......no.
No.
No no no no no no no no no no no no no no no.
Aren't you something?"

WINTER CURE

When the shoulders slouch and the heart
is low during a Pro Tools or neighbor noise morning,
take the gamble to throw your head and shoulders
back and put
your face in the sun and reconnoiter your fancy
free through orange eyelid worms.
If that does not cure, put your moon there
and get your ass warmed. Get it burnt, even
Let your
wind blow, legs stretching, feet
planted, hands digging for the devil
that gave you such a spine
to stand alongside the traffic
belching that mushroom cloud.

MILLIONAIRE TURF

A friend has a hole in her heart
and wants to fill it with baby teeth.
Is that even a thing?
She said she filled it with shoes,
but it didn't do the trick.

Anyway, there is a cyber call to help her out
(she is in a state; was up all night
digging those shoes out of there)
the ever-tapping concerned suggest
it is gonna take a fuck ton
of teeth to do the trick.

Some summer evenings
the cicadas think
they are impervious
if a dolphin in the bathtub
says that the umlaut
is the clitoris of language
and nipples are weeping,
but failure is in the swelling of joints
and the nightmares of sparse crowds
breaking into fights amidst the sublime.

Failure is in the faces of heroes and friends.
Their loss is swirling down the drains of the angelic,
too busy to deal with the mess
of the bored' attempts
to kill time.

Goalposts and millionaire turf, amped
but nervous despite an overwhelming
sense of despair in the street.
Stuffing cabbage under caps in
fear of a collapse leaves guilt trip
ween off need, but waste energy
sprinting after shots
behind the curtains
of aldermanic fellatio
and bounced check swings
of a homeless guy
in nice sneakers
just in time
for a new CVS
sidewalk nap after Midnight.

Ears are ringing.
Someone is thinking of
She and him and then
He busts out laughing.
Ha! HA! Ha!!!
"She and him make a shim!"
Ha!

Meanwhile, wars are singing.
Give something, Millionaire Janitor,
seeking pleasure
and weird, beautiful, functional
suitable vacancy unlike affordable
housing.

Reusable shopping underwear
stolen people get lost,
fostering a rabbit quickly with little effort
calls for service stem from things like prostitution,
coloring outside the lines, shootings,
drug underdoses and "actually"
just assaults.

You just can't quite get deep enough,
but you can bang the hell out of the sides.
Try not to worry too much.
Mismatched energy is kind.
Things devolve
into the problem you're facing.

Gallons and gallons of spaghetti
sauce with Fred Rogers
hovering over your bedhead
under the memory
of tree limbs and yard waste
freedom and secret thoughts
of love and hatred.

Get the performance
you're looking for, smiling Victim.
For the out-of-town
to be nimble and keep art
fart smell of raw nature
is more bewildering,
but, could tell you what it is?
Nothing compared to it.
Maybe weed.

Beautiful, heavy
a cold, wet fig?
Good night, Poet.

There is a boy's drawing of a golden peacock
Despite the woman saying "no" to him,
he continued to ask her questions
and pet her cat.

Everclear some foliage charges, say,
"That's not a question."
Wildly into the woods, passing the naked
William and the book
Snacking and competing
and not just trying.
Sit down…and figure out what's next.

A friend has a hole in her heart
and wants to fill it with baby teeth.
Is that even a thing?
She said she filled it with shoes,
but it didn't do the trick.
Anyway, there is a cyber call to help her out
(she is in a state; was up all night
digging those shoes out of there)
the ever-tapping concerned suggest
it is gonna take a fuck ton
of teeth to do the trick.
Who is your kid's orthodontist?
Also, can a cactus own a duck?

Is that a diving board off to the left?
Must've been a moth in a peripheral
need for dreams.
Hammocks are best suggesting
we all take a chill pill and hang loose
inclined to say no to Choppy surf
waffles and old-school death.
Use insurance Wipes to erase
corpses.

Giving you cookies is nothing new
packed with trinkets
deeply annoying
dream phrase pops
genitalia on the copier
before they actually do it.

No explanations, no reviews.
Mostly cloudy perceptions and thoughts
excited to take the first hop.
That's it for today!!
Goodbye, Grasshoppers!!!

Yearn to be at peace flanked by a tactical unit
with all the junk heads ending America's
innocence.

Tarzan speaks art outside in the splash pad,
into some torn security blanket
and dusty toys and books,
or so the reports say.

So, I'm gonna be lazy and ask you instead
of google where this took place to vote
on the gun bill chain letter assault
on another woman who was walking
her dog and you die to vote
on the control bill chain letter
known suffering, known struggle, known loss:
stoned just like our breadsticks
into some torn security blanket
playing ping pong in the Andes.

That is what happens when you meet a Nazi in the AlpS.
translated in Google and a cherished Cockatoo,
Lopglop bingbop, and friends massing on the jungle gym.
Is there an echo in here?

It's weird when people seek pleasure and beautiful,
functional, suitable coffin space pain
translated in Google and a cherished Cockatoo,
Lopglop bingbop, and friends massing
on the jungle gym.

Become a stenographer to the appropriate person
terrified by the local wise woman's triple prophecy:
Donny's suicide;
McKee's wussy exposed;
Sinquefield impaled on a horny bishop
wouldn't know what to do
with this her perforated love muscle;
Not even with a broken-down trolley
full of baby teeth.

FAITH

She saw a dog puppet licking the branch outside her
    window
She had 17 girly, vodka drinks and a bottle of wine
painted naked in acrylic all night long
Later that afternoon the dog puppet
dissolved into pain

THE PERFECT

Meggy was a cutter but damn she was fine
99 tear drops and half a case of wine
A bucket of vices and a box of parking tickets
A bevy of boyfriends, she said, died with the rickets.
I didn't believe her
I didn't have to
She didn't expect much
Gauze, tape and a screw
And
    that's
        about
           all
              she
                  got.

NIBLETS

Her neighbors thought she was pleasant.
Her lover assumed she would stay.
She fell asleep to the Travel Channel
despising Rachel Ray.
Awake: she thought earlobes sounded delicious
but hobbled to the market
for pig's feet.

BREJANETT MIX

"Piss, interesting development, piss is now okay on television if you're pissed off, but not if you're pissed on. In other words, if you change the preposition you get in trouble. It's alright for me to say to you 'why are you pissed off at me?' But you can't say 'because you pissed on me.'"

-George Carlin

Red masks, with white embroidered letters placed on dogs.

This isn't your typical wedding.

Standing six feet away is the truth you seek.

Remember to freeze some piss. You'll miss it when

    it's gone.

If a person doesn't know what it's like to suffer

the loss of a father or the loss of R. Kelly,

they know not the smell of clean sheets.

BUDDHA BUSSED TABLES

Aunt Bee be more worried and so and so
and then some more than usual,
which is really say say say
saying something but nothing
and so and so and then some!

The good news is that your worries
might inspire a positive effect
for the billing professionals,
so think hard and sleep soft
and then get busy or dizzy
and so and weave and sew
and so and then some more worries.

You and ewes could be more worried
and so and so and then some
more than usual,
which is really saying something
and so and so and then some!
The good news is that your worries
might inspire a positive effect,
so think hard and then get busy
or dizzy and so and weave
and sew and so and then some
more worrisome sum
of the worrisome make it happen.

You can happen in the Target
parking lot on Hampton
thinking about Fred Hampton.

Don't flatter yourself.
Trios on a rainbow
never take a shit at Hardee's
without spending at least morphine
in the mind's eye.
Buddha stumbled in and bussed tables
got accidentally coked up and splooged
all over Eve's McRib
in a teenage pop-punk band with him
in New Jersey.

ENVISION LIGHT

Still in socks on a November night,
but the computer blows warm air
on legs and the hood is over head
as it bows over
a poem about ex-girlfriends
becoming strangers and the disruptive
and powerful forces of change
and then comes a fruit fly in search
of the missing whiskey glass
that should be on the desk.
The little fucker foolishly lands on page 5
and crawls towards the left margin.
I crush it there, re-open the book
and turn the page.

In a few minutes, the computer crashes
and it is time scribbled into the script
before the director closes the set
for another take. Another scene.
to hit the streets for the missing whiskey.

Nothing is certain.
Still time to talk to the dead
and whatever life can be.

Oh, take it back to a land of forgiveness
and hope where limbs break
under the weight of nooses
and become wings.

Where tweets of anger beget
wisdom and urgency sleeps
in siestas in a warm breeze and bullets
turn into fleas that buzz music
in golden rays.

Where open eyes envision light
and gravity lapses into strength.

SELECT ACTION

Steps hits the streets every Mundayne
mined clarity from sleeping minds
spun piecemeal wheels healing
in dreck of a slim paycheck
for something as divine
as vanishing points
of light in a better
way of living
and to fool
them with
squinted
third
eye.

Brett Lars Underwood is a St. Louis poet and promoter. He is the author of *MUSH* (SPARTAN PRESS, 2018) and *MUSHARONA* (Kung Fu Treachery Press, 2020). His verse and riddles have been published by *Poetrybay, 52nd City, Curator Magazine* and included in *FLOOD STAGE: An Anthology of Saint Louis Poets, The Gasconade Review presents 39 Feet and Rising, Missouri is a Ghost-Shaped Thing* and *After the Flood* (Spartan Press, 2019). His work has been heard at the Pulitzer Foundation for the Arts SOUND WAVES series and with the HEARDING CATS COLLECTIVE. He is the former host of THE NO SHOW (KDHX 88.1 FM, 2000-07) He is currently hosting the podcast, HIGH ABOVE GRAND (Spotify, Audible and other major platforms), interviewing St. Louis poets. He can be reached at brettlarsunderwood@gmail.com

This project was made possible, in part, by generous support from the Osage Arts Community.

Osage Arts Community provides temporary time, space and support for the creation of new artistic works in a retreat format, serving creative people of all kinds — visual artists, composers, poets, fiction and nonfiction writers. Located on a 152-acre farm in an isolated rural mountainside setting in Central Missouri and bordered by ¾ of a mile of the Gasconade River, OAC provides residencies to those working alone, as well as welcoming collaborative teams, offering living space and workspace in a country environment to emerging and mid-career artists. For more information, visit us at www.osageac.org

Osage Arts Community